Advance Praise for *Stragility*

"If you could translate the learning from decades of experience building flexible and responsive organizations into a toolkit for change leaders at all levels, you'd have Auster and Hillenbrand's *Stragility*. As I read this book, I kept thinking 'I've got to get copies of this book for my colleagues!' *Stragility* is a treasure trove of practical tools for rapidly engaging and aligning your organization to execute your strategy."

Andrew Atkins, Chief Innovation Officer, Interaction Associates

"Auster and Hillenbrand understand how change works in the real world. Every business leader should read this book and commit it to memory."

R. Edward Freeman, University Professor,
Darden School of Business, University of Virginia

"*Stragility* is brilliant. Learning to excel at leading change is increasingly the most critical foundational skill for leaders at all levels of the organization and across industries. Banks who will win tomorrow are the ones who would have adopted the mindset of *Stragility* – to navigate current change challenges while building change skills and resiliency. I recommend this book to anyone looking at how to succeed in shaping the future of their company and adapting to the new reality."

Rebecca Kehat, Executive Vice President, Head of Strategy &
Marketing, Retail Division, Bank Hapoalim, Israel

"Without the right approach to strategy and implementation, no company can achieve its fullest potential. *Stragility* is the compass to navigating your team across the choppy waters of change. Fast-paced, riveting, powerful ... a brilliant book by two global thought leaders!"

Krissi Barr, President, Barr Corporate Success

"*Stragility* stands out as the one book on strategic change that helps the reader navigate the surprising realities encountered once execution gets underway. It provides a highly effective series of diagnostic tools, action step proposals and templates that help one recognize if course corrections are needed, how they should look, and how to manage the political realities. Finally, *Stragility* provides suggestions for staying ahead of competition for the long-term."

Wolfgang Berndt, Deputy Chairman of the Board, OMV AG, Vienna, Austria

"With clients all over the world, I am only sorry not to have had these perspectives and practical suggestions in my tool box years ago! *Stragility* shows us that ultimate business success lies at the cross-roads of the Sticky Strategies from the top and Leadership Agility at all levels!"

Bob Lank, Nikoleta & Associates

"If I was putting together the dream team of organizational change experts, Ellen Auster and Lisa Hillenbrand would be my first picks. They know how to develop and lead organizational level change in a way that works and leaves the organization stronger. This book is a must read for managers hoping to do the same."

George Carey, CEO, The Family Room

"In any organization, change starts with a strategy, but it doesn't happen just because leaders declare it. There must be a critical mass of support at the top and organization engagement top to bottom so that strategies are turned into concrete actions. Auster and Hillenbrand offer practical, easy-to-apply guidance to activate change. It's a quick must-read."

Charlotte Otto, retired Global External Relations Officer, Procter & Gamble

"*Stragility* had me ripping through my own organization and immediately mapping the lessons inside to our challenges. Want to sidestep landmines, own the best opportunities and strike fear into the hearts of your competitors? *Stragility* is a necessary read for every entrepreneur who is working to create disruptive dynamo."

Joe Diubaldo, President, Clarity Recruitment

"Every page and paragraph shares inside stories of known organizations and tools with findings that are applicable to all leaders, from emerging entrepreneurs to Fortune 100 leaders. The fundamental focus on the role and power of people is timely as shifting workforces and flexible workplaces challenge conventional strategies. I am excited to introduce these strategic, agile and people-powered tools to our leadership team, alliance partners and clients."

Lisa Taylor, President, Challenge Factory

"Many leaders believe that change is a matter of direction setting. Ellen Auster and Lisa Hillenbrand know from their personal experiences that direction-setting is only the beginning and, frankly, the easiest part of the journey. They synthesize the practical actions that leaders can take to move themselves and others through change, and, importantly, to make change stick! They have managed to define straightforward lessons from their successful careers in fostering change and extracting simplicity across complex organizations and stakeholders."

Joan M. Lewis, Board of Directors, comScore, Inc.

"*Stragility* expertly underscores the truism that execution eats strategy for lunch. This book shows that the best transformation strategies have well-thought-out implementation plans that fully consider a company's culture, willingness to change, its key internal influencers, as well as anticipating barriers with focused and pragmatic plans to overcome them."

Frank Ruppen, Founder, Forward Associates

"In this volatile world, analysis paralysis kills. Lisa Hillenbrand and Ellen Auster have captured great stories and very easy diagnostic grids that allow you ponder and move without blunder. This book is a must for any learning organization."

Laston Charriez, Senior Vice President, Marketing Product
and Market Development, Western Union

"Finally, a book on making change happen. In the technology world, winning requires a nimble organization working several generations ahead. *Stragility* is a fantastic roadmap for organization change. Wish I'd had it years ago!"

Vince Hudson, Vice President of Marketing Strategy
and Operations, Samsung Electronics USA

"*Stragility* is *the* guidebook that will equip emerging leaders to consciously build a more change-capable organization. It is full of powerful tools, concepts, and stories that will help emerging talent take on complex, top priority work and succeed."

Ashley Hilkewich, Pathways to Education Canada;
Canada's Most Powerful Women: Top 100 – Future Leader

Stragility

EXCELLING AT STRATEGIC CHANGES

ELLEN R. AUSTER | LISA HILLENBRAND

UNIVERSITY OF TORONTO PRESS
Toronto Buffalo London

© Ellen R. Auster and Lisa Hillenbrand 2016
Rotman-UTP Publishing
Toronto Buffalo London
www.utppublishing.com
Printed in Canada

ISBN 978-1-4426-4805-0

♾ Printed on acid-free, 100% post-consumer recycled paper with
vegetable-based inks.

Library and Archives Canada Cataloguing in Publication

Auster, Ellen R., author
Stragility : excelling at strategic changes / Ellen R. Auster and Lisa Hillenbrand.

Includes bibliographical references and index.
ISBN 978-1-4426-4805-0 (bound)

1. Organizational change.   2. Strategic planning.   3. Leadership.
I. Hillenbrand, Lisa, 1957–, author   II. Title.

HD58.8.A98 2016   658.4'06   C2015-907178-X

University of Toronto Press acknowledges the financial assistance to its publishing
program of the Canada Council for the Arts and the Ontario Arts Council, an
agency of the Government of Ontario.

 Canada Council **Conseil des Arts**
for the Arts **du Canada**

 ONTARIO ARTS COUNCIL
CONSEIL DES ARTS DE L'ONTARIO
an Ontario government agency
un organisme du gouvernement de l'Ontario

Funded by the   Financé par le
Government   gouvernement
of Canada   du Canada

To my amazing daughters Shannon and Lindsey Auster-Weiss and Kristen Tingue, and my wonderful parents, Don and Nancy Auster. For all your love and for teaching me personal Stragility.

Ellen R. Auster

For Adam and Helen Jatho. You have been the best changes in my life. Watching you grow and expertly navigate all life's ups and downs fills me with pride and joy.

Lisa Hillenbrand

Contents

Acknowledgments

There are many people who supported us and helped make this book a reality. We want to start by thanking our colleagues, clients, and thought leaders everywhere for their insights and impact on our thinking. We so appreciate the fantastic MBA, EMBA, and PhD students, change leaders, and clients that Ellen has taught and worked with over the years. They have test-run many earlier versions of the ideas and tools in this book in their own organizations, and we thank them for their feedback and for sharing their stories.

We are grateful to Shannon Auster-Weiss for her inspirational contributions, sparking and shaping our ideas with her research, input, and story gathering in the early stages of our writing. Bori Csillag was terrific with her help with initial framing of the content. Thanks to Steve Weiss for tolerating our Post-it Notes and flip charts all around the living room and our excitement as we drafted various chapters on our week-long writing immersions. Teresa Back was marvelous in her handling and assistance with manuscript preparation, including internal design, figures, and references. Brenda Zimmerman opened our minds years ago to the power of complexity thinking and was a great sounding board for thinking about how her ideas of paradox, going with good enough, distributed ownership, and preventing "snap back" connect to our work. Lindsey Auster-Weiss provided exceptional facilitation and feedback during cover design, framework fine-tuning, and the page proof process.

At Procter & Gamble, Lisa is grateful for outstanding mentors and colleagues including John Pepper, A.G. Lafley, Bob McDonald, Wolfgang Berndt, Deb Henretta, Charlotte Otto, Paul Polman, Claudia Kotchka, Jim Stengel, Joan Lewis, Leonora Polonsky, Dina Howell, Matt Carcieri, Suzanne Tosolini, Frank Ruppen, Gibby Carey, Rad Ewing, Ute Hagen, Pauline Manos, Lisa Napolione, Cindy Tripp, and Karen Van

Wagenen. Thanks to the thousands of brand teams Lisa has worked with over the years. What a rich collection of learnings to draw from! Procter & Gamble really is the best brand-building company in the world.

It has been our pleasure to work with the team at Rotman-UTP Publishing. Jennifer DiDomenico was fabulous as she deftly navigated the publishing process with us. Roger Martin provided vital feedback on an early précis of the book. Val Cooke was creative with interior design, and Leah Connor and Barbie Halaby were excellent with copy-editing. Thank you to Steve Arenburg and Ken McGuffin from the Rotman School of Management for their support and ideas.

We are indebted to and have learned so much from our families. We want to thank our parents – Don and Nancy Auster and Bernard Hillenbrand, Aliceann Wohlbruck, Liz Hillenbrand, and Michael Fishman – for giving us drive and encouragement to pursue our dreams. Their optimism and perseverance as they have faced the ups and downs of their lives is truly remarkable Stragility. Thanks to our siblings Carol Auster, John Hillenbrand, Susan Hillenbrand Avallon, and Laura Hillenbrand and to our dear friends Lesley Simpson, Alan Schwartz, Liz Denton, Julie Fox, and Ruth Parks.

Our children, Lindsey and Shannon Auster-Weiss, and Kristen and Derrick Tingue, and Helen and Adam Jatho, and grandchildren, Ada and Rafe Tingue, provided ongoing support throughout the process. Each of them has taught us how to be present and how to navigate change in the most magnificent and delightful ways. Thank you for letting us try out many of the ideas in this book on you. We also would like to acknowledge Zippee, Shoji, Chip, Biscuit, and Mia for keeping us grounded.

Finally, we are both grateful for the most superb and joyful coauthoring experience ever. We applied many of the principles in this book to our writing process. We discovered the power of strong collaboration, friendship, and love to create a "better together" book. And we had a lot of fun in the process. It reinforced to us that it really is a better way to work and to live.

chapter one

Stragility – Strategic, Agile, People-Powered Change

*Change is the norm. To be sure, it is painful and risky, and above all it
requires a great deal of very hard work. But unless it is seen as the task
of the organization to lead change, the organization – whether business,
university, hospital and so on – will not survive. In a period of rapid
structural change, the only ones who survive are the Change Leaders.*

Peter Drucker[1]

Change Is Everywhere and All the Time

No matter what job title and company appear on our business cards, the ability to translate strategy into action and lead strategic change successfully is an essential skill for both personal and organizational success. Increasing global competition, rapid technological advances, unpredictable economic forces, and demanding customers all mean that change is constant in today's fast-paced business environment.

Current strategic challenges on our plate might include expanding to new markets, offering a new type of product or service to customers, integrating a recently acquired company, improving product innovation, or restructuring departments, functions, or whole companies. Being an effective leader requires juggling multiple change initiatives simultaneously and succeeding in leading change day in and day out. Even if our business is doing well now, standing still in today's world is impossible. For a company to succeed, it needs to embrace rapid change and be nimble in the face of disruptive macro trends and hyper-competition. The need for change never stops. To survive or, better yet, thrive, we need to keep transforming our organizations again and again.

Easy to Say, Hard to Do

For many of us, that's easy to say but hard to do. We've been asked to turn around a weak department or division, shut down an operation, merge several departments, launch a new approach, or re-engineer a whole system. And through it all we're downsizing, trying to hit ever increasing growth targets and cope with turbulence generated by competitors, technology, social trends, or political and economic turmoil. It seems an impossible task. We're feeling like Sisyphus forever pushing boulders up a hill only to watch them roll right back down again.

We're doing the best we can. But we're under constant time pressure. Quarterly results are staring us in the face. We're juggling way too many projects and initiatives, with too few people to do all the work. External forces are pummeling us and we have a hard time doing anything but firefighting. So we tell 'em what to do, shovel politics under the rug, work longer and longer hours, and pray it will all somehow work out. If we're lucky, some of our projects and initiatives are moving along OK. But others are likely derailing and probably a few are flatlining. We may also often feel powerless in the face of the soft side of change – the politics, the emotions, and the massive work involved that keeps so many of us and those we work with in a constant state of exhaustion.

We know we're operating at subpar levels. We're struggling to stay positive as our anxiety and stress mount. We're not sure we have the right strategy with market forces always shifting. We know our employees are disengaged. We know the politics are poisoning what we're doing. We know everyone is exhausted and maxed out and we can't keep doing what we're doing.

Change is hard at the individual level, but it gets even harder across organizations. Translating strategy into action is not easy. Tragically, more than 70 percent of change efforts fail and in most cases the organization emerges weaker – exhausted, demoralized, and confused – and less able to take on the next round of change initiatives.[2] The answer can't be that we all need to stop changing. As Jack Welch said, "If the rate of change on the outside exceeds the rate of change on the inside, the end is near."[3] Sadly, in most changes, much more attention is paid to the plan, costs, and investments than to the people who have to make a change work.

So how can we increase our odds of change success for the strategic challenges we have on our plate now and those we'll inevitably face in the future?

Introducing Stragility – Strategic, Agile, People-Powered Change

"Stragility" is our term for strategic, agile, people-powered change that enables our organizations to thrive amidst relentless turbulence and uncertainty. Achieving Stragility is the key to competitive advantage that lasts. Whether we're making a major change in strategic direction or course-correcting a strategy already in the works, we need Stragility to harness the energy and ideas of our people to accomplish key goals today. And we need it to build the necessary change capabilities to enable us to continually rally to meet the next change on the horizon.

STRAGILITY = STRATEGIC, AGILE, PEOPLE-POWERED CHANGE

Roger Federer: Shifting Both Strategies and Execution to Win

Tennis champion Roger Federer has just lost the first set of a critical match. What does he think about in those few minutes before he has to get back out on the court? Does he just take a few deep breaths and "try harder," like Sisyphus pushing the same rock up the same hill? He told an interviewer recently that he asks himself two key questions:

- *Is there something in my strategy I need to change?* Maybe he anticipated his opponent would stay on the baseline and he's coming to net more than expected. Maybe an old injury is flaring up, which necessitates a modification in his game plan.

- *Am I just not executing the strategy effectively?* Maybe a few close shots went long because they didn't have enough topspin. Maybe he didn't put enough force into his first serve. In those cases, he reassures himself that the strategy is right and thinks about how he can execute better and fine-tune his game.

Just like Federer, we must constantly adjust both strategies and execution to meet winning goals. That agility is a key part of Stragility. Leaders cannot set strategy or execution once and forget it. Without ongoing agility, even good strategies will fail. And Stragility is not just something done by top management or leaders. Every individual is making decisions constantly that either support or get in the way of effective strategy execution. Sometimes when we hit slumps, the change requires a modification to the strategy, and sometimes the devil is in the implementation details. We must ensure our change efforts are rooted in clear strategies about where to play and how to win *and* we must be able to secure the commitment of the organization to make them happen. A.G. Lafley, Procter & Gamble's CEO, who came out of retirement to lead the company through a turnaround, expresses the demands well: "On the one hand, it is about winning with shoppers and customers in the marketplace. On the other hand it is about engagement and ownership and personal accountability. Change requires real emotional and personal commitment and a lot of energy and personal action. We all need to put ourselves on the line to do it."[4]

Many approaches overlook the importance of grounding change in a strategic context and instead tend to look at change as a discrete process that begins and ends. In addition, they typically emphasize large-scale transformational change accomplished predominantly by top management, and gloss over key soft aspects of change such as sparking people's passion, overcoming the politics and emotions, and preventing the change fatigue that can paralyze even the best people.

In contrast, Stragility is useful for any type of change, at any point in a change process, and for building change fitness. Stragility will help you nurture and cultivate a change-capable organization. Instead of going it alone, you'll be able to harness the talents and potential of those you work with to make positive change happen. Stragility will enable you to successfully tackle the change challenges you face now and simultaneously build the change capabilities you need to address future strategic shifts. We'll also provide action steps to enable you and those you work with to create winning change again and again, more easily and with less work.

Both of us (the authors) have felt the same pressures you do. We have worked in and with organizations trying to turn around results. We've spent sleepless nights with clients trying to sketch out a plan and then faced the blank stares from overwhelmed colleagues who are not sure how to move forward. We've seen the best strategies derail because of politics, inaction, or incompatibility with systems and processes. And we've felt the burden of trying to move forward without the support of others.

We've consolidated everything we've learned from our own trial-and-error experiences, from mentors, from academic research, from our consulting practices, and from successful business executives to help you avoid the pitfalls and master the art of Stragility. We offer four key Stragility skills and their related success principles, which we have found to be the most useful in enabling individuals and organizations to get better at change and achieve both the major shifts and the minor pivots needed to transform again and again. We've used these Stragility skills and applied these success principles to our businesses, our consulting practice, our social-sector work, and, yes, even our personal lives. They've helped us and others deal with un-discussable subjects like politics and overwrought emotions. Armed with these skills and success principles, we've worked with leaders across many different industries and organizations to tackle the challenges they face now and build Stragility in their organizations.

Before we move on, we want to note how we are using the words "we" and "organization." The pronoun "we" is used throughout the book in two ways. Most of the time, "we" refers to all of us as change practitioners who together are constantly learning. There are also instances where "we" refers to us, the authors, and our point of view or experience. An example would be when we highlight a project we've worked on together. We'll denote that with "(the authors)" as we did two paragraphs earlier.

Second, the word "organization" refers to the organizational unit most relevant to you. It might be your immediate team, your department or division, or your region or the entire organization. It will likely vary depending on the particular change challenge you are tackling and your role in the organization.

Stragility Skills

Figure 1.1 captures the four Stragility skills that form the foundation of our approach and that we'll be building on throughout the book. Each chapter is devoted to understanding and working through one of these four skills critical for Stragility.

Figure 1.1: Four critical Stragility skills

STRAGILITY SKILL: SENSE AND SHIFT STRATEGY TO WIN
Worried your strategy is off track? Or feel like you may have locked and loaded on a strategy that no longer makes sense? Chapter 2, "Redefining Strategy to Win," provides tips that will enable you to systematically sense whether shifts in strategy are needed and to redefine your strategy to beat the competition in a dynamic world. This chapter also covers how to gauge whether course corrections are desirable for internal systems and structures to bring those strategies to life.

STRAGILITY SKILL: EMBRACE OUR INNER POLITICIAN
Don't know how to address those thorny political issues? The politics of change are typically ignored, but they can fester, wreak havoc, and derail even the best-laid plans. In chapter 3, "Building Support," we give you a proactive approach for navigating the politics and emotions. You'll learn how to leverage

the ideas, skills, and passion of sponsors and promoters and transform the concerns and fears of fence-sitters and skeptics into ideas and commitment for every change you lead.

STRAGILITY SKILL: INSPIRE AND ENGAGE

Tired of force-feeding change and facing apathy or resistance? Chapter 4, "Fostering Ownership and Accountability," walks you through how to roll out the change in an inclusive, two-way, high-touch manner that will cultivate shared ownership and win hearts and minds.

STRAGILITY SKILL: CHANGE FITNESS

Too worn out with no time for any of this? Sure, there might be a better way but most of us are so exhausted we're just trying to get through the day. We are juggling multiple change initiatives simultaneously. And making strategy come alive with burned-out, demoralized, exhausted teams is difficult if not impossible. In chapter 5, "Creating Successful Change Again and Again," we'll offer new tips and tools for transforming change fatigue into the change fitness that will give your organization the capabilities and resilience to flourish in a world that never stops.

Mastering these four Stragility skills will help you increase your organization's odds of not only surviving change but also thriving as you work toward accomplishing your goals. In the process, you'll be developing one of the strongest sources of competitive advantage out there: the ability to navigate current change challenges while building the long-run change capabilities needed for ongoing success in unpredictable and stormy external contexts.

Change is difficult, both personally and organizationally. Applying the proven principles and practices from this book will make it easier. And you will get better with each change effort. As a former CEO of a Fortune 50 company says,

> Coping with change is like learning anything new – a new workout routine, a new diet, a new golf swing, a new job. At first it's really hard. It feels unnatural and requires lots of effort. Sometimes you give up and go back to the old way of doing things. But if you keep at it, over time what was once new becomes easier

and easier until it's almost second nature. I was accustomed to change. I'd been through enough change to know that good can always come out of it, so I could see the opportunity and the possibilities.[5]

How to Use This Book

Here are some tips on how to use this book. First, don't feel you have to read the book from front to back. Begin where it makes the most sense given the change challenges you are facing right now. The Stragility Diagnostic Tool in the following table will help you assess where you are and what help you might need. It provides a summary of some of the biggest bad habits and the pain points or symptoms associated with these habits (as shown on the left of the table). On the right of the table are the Stragility goals and Stragility skills that can transform this pain into successful change. This diagnostic can help you identify what chapters you might want to start with given the change challenges you currently have in the works or are about to face.

If you feel like your strategy is derailing and you're in a downward spiral, you might start with chapter 2. If change is rife with political issues and is emotionally charged, take a look at chapter 3 and how to embrace your inner politician. Maybe everyone is giving the change lip service but not really engaged. If so, then chapter 4 might be where you dive in. You could even start at the end in chapter 5 and work your way backward if change fatigue and burnout is what keeps you up at night.

No matter where you start, we suggest that eventually you work through the entire book. While every change challenge is unique and will require change leaders to emphasize each of these dimensions to a greater or lesser degree, creating Stragility in your organization requires the skills and capabilities embedded in all four principles. Only then will your organization be equipped to effectively and efficiently handle any type of change challenge and to tackle change again and again.

In the next four chapters, we drill down on our four key Stragility skills to help you make the pain go away and win every time. We begin each chapter with an "At a Glance" section that provides a snapshot of the Stragility success principles associated with each Stragility skill. We've included lots of real-life stories of how others have tackled these same

STRAGILITY DIAGNOSTIC TOOL 1-1:
PAIN POINTS, BAD HABITS, GOALS, AND SKILLS

Read the whole book or look for pain points, bad habits, or strategic goals that resonate and begin there.

Pain Points	Bad Habit	Stragility Goal	Stragility Skill
Downward spirals, blindsided, strategic drift, underutilized capabilities	Lock and Load	Redefining Strategy to Win	Chapter 2: Sense and Shift
Political infighting, turf wars, resistance, apathy	Ignore the Politics	Building Support	Chapter 3: Embrace Our Inner Politician
Disengagement, blaming, inaction, resentment	Tell and Sell	Fostering Ownership and Accountability	Chapter 4: Inspire and Engage
Exhaustion, stress, burnout, wasted money, time, and resources	Change Fatigue	Creating Successful Change Again and Again	Chapter 5: Change Fitness

challenges and succeeded in bringing Stragility to life in their organizations. We end each chapter with a specific Stragility diagnostic related to that Stragility skill that will enable you to focus and choose which tools address what's most pressing for you. Each of these Stragility tools will help you conduct the necessary analyses to generate concrete action steps and drill down on the details. This practical, action-oriented approach will enable you to leverage your strengths, tackle your pain points, and achieve your desired strategic goals while developing the Stragility skills, capabilities, and fitness necessary for long-term competitive advantage in a world that's always changing.

chapter two

Redefining Strategy to Win:
From Lock and Load to
Sense and Shift

Stragility Skill

Sense and Shift

Stragility Success Principles

Redefine Winning
- Define purpose and mission
- Choose metrics that matter

Watch Our Wings
- Anticipate game-changing forces
- Get granular
- Be a market maker

Align Internal Capabilities
- Leverage strengths
- Address pain points

Shift Strategies and Tactics
- Backcast the future
- Make best this-day-forward decision
- Ask what would have to be true

*Strategy is about making choices, trade-offs; it's about deliberately
choosing to be different.*

Michael Porter[1]

Redefining strategy to win is the first skill necessary for Stragility. Strategy is not something we can develop once and forget. It needs to be constantly fine-tuned not just at the top of the company but all the way from the front-line people to the CEO. It helps to know our end goal, but it is impossible to follow a 3- to 5-year plan in a dynamic marketplace. So while it might be tempting to "lock and load" the strategy and then mentally walk away, that's typically not a good idea.

As Pepsi CEO Indra Nooyi attests, "There is nothing like a concrete life plan to weigh you down. Because if you always have one eye on some future goal, you stop paying attention to the job at hand, miss opportunities that might arise, and stay fixedly on one path, even when a better, newer course might have opened up."[2]

We might end up with a poorly delivered strategy because no one is clear on purpose, mission, or metrics, or get blindsided by changes in the marketplace, or miss the next big opportunity that shapes our industry. We might fail to do the regular internal checkups and check-ins that enable us to leverage our strengths and address pain points. We might find ourselves with change that's stalled because we're drowning in sunk costs and failures and not investing enough in what is working.

When we are confronted with challenges like these, we have the same dilemmas tennis star Roger Federer faces when he has lost the first set and is assessing whether the strategy or execution need adjusting to win.

So what might help us? In their business bestseller, *Playing to Win*, P&G CEO A.G. Lafley and thought leader and former dean of the Rotman School of Management at University of Toronto Roger Martin discuss strategy as five critical nested choices: Winning Aspiration, Where to Play, How to Win, Capabilities, and Systems.[3] We believe that assessing and shifting these sets of choices is critical to any successful change. In this book, we're not going to focus on how to create strategy. You're the expert in your industry, and Lafley and Martin's book tackles this issue brilliantly. Instead, this chapter will offer you tips and tools you can use to sense when strategy is veering off track and or when internal systems, structure, and processes are ineffective at bringing a smart strategy to life.

Macy's: Redefining Strategy Leads to Record Growth

Macy's CEO and "Chief Customer Officer" Terry Lundgren likes to tell the story of his early career experience as the dinnerware buyer for 20 stores. At the time, he knew every store manager, the top sales associates, and what sold and didn't sell in each store. If one store needed 20 Lenox china sets in time for a bride's wedding, he would search until he found the sets and personally deliver them to the store that was selling them to the bride. After many mergers – with Bloomingdale's, Lazarus, Filene's, and Marshall Fields – Macy's realized that they were not winning because they had gotten out of touch with local stores and their customers. Lundgren longed to find a way back to the kind of local understanding he had as a young store manager. The vision was clear: balance localization and scale in a way that brought back and enhanced the magic of Macy's. So, armed with this commitment to reinvent the store by getting back to their roots, they tested a more localized concept at their 20 worst-performing stores. When it worked, they expanded their new strategy nationally.

Macy's captured the essence of changes they wanted in their "MOM strategy": MOM = My Macy's, Omnichannel, and Magic Selling:

My Macy's – Tailored product offerings in each store and local taste (what customers in Miami want is different from those in Cincinnati) that are so well chosen that each customer feels like this is her or his Macy's.
Omnichannel – Make it easy for customers to shop anywhere, anytime, and on any device.
Magic Selling – No matter where customers shop, the customer interaction is at the center of all they do.

"Everyone's job changed, including my own," Lundgren recalls.[4] To personalize this strategy, they encouraged employees to "Be the Magic" and offered training designed to help them with concrete ways to do that. For example, when a customer returned an item, they were welcomed back and helped to find something more suitable.

Redefine Winning

Too often companies and organizations get off track chasing growth or profit or volume without being clear what winning means. Like other best-practice companies, Macy's shift to the MOM strategy wasn't the only time they've sensed that things were going off-kilter and revamped and reinvented. They've continued to shift and refine their strategy to win in multiple channels. A typical Macy's customer will use the search function to find an item, come in and try it out, check out ratings and reviews on social media, and then buy it from their mobile device. Macy's has invested significant resources to ensure that this type of magical experience is synergistic across all their consumer touchpoints. By delineating a clear strategy, shifting to reflect a changed landscape, and continually monitoring trends, they are a rare department store that not only has survived but has actually sustained competitive advantage over the past several years, with most earnings quarters beating expectations.

Define Purpose and Mission

It all starts with an external focus on winning in the marketplace with the customers or clients who matter most.

When A.G. Lafley first became CEO of Procter & Gamble in 2000, he created the "Consumer Is Boss" mantra. He was very clear that the consumer was at the center of P&G's strategy. As he said, "P&G's purpose is to touch and improve more consumers' lives with more P&G brands and products every day. Of all our stakeholders, both outside and inside, the primary one is the consumer."[5] This led to new measures of consumer satisfaction, a focus on the first moment of truth (the store) and the second moment of truth (when consumers use the products).

Returning to P&G in 2013, he and his team adjusted the strategy again after multiple acquisitions resulted in too many smaller brands, not all of which were good fits with the company's core competencies. Realizing that P&G had gotten too big, Lafley announced in 2014 that P&G would sell or discontinue about 50 percent of the brands to increase focus on the big ones.

"This is a classic strategic choice," Lafley said during a conference call with analysts on 1 August 2014. "We want to be in the businesses we should be in, not the businesses we are in ... The 70 to 80 core brands that P&G plans to retain account for 90 percent of sales and more than 95 percent of profits." More recently he said, "We will become a much more focused, much more streamlined company. We are going to create a faster-growing, more-profitable company that's far simpler to manage and operate. This will enable P&G people to be more agile and responsive, more flexible and faster. Less will be much more."[6]

Like Macy's and P&G, every organization needs to regularly redefine strategy, focusing the organization on winning in the marketplace in light of changes in the external environment.

Choose Metrics That Matter

As we adjust strategies, we also need to alter our metrics to focus on those that drive our desired outcomes. This requires thinking about what combination of outcome-focused measures (market share), lead measures that are early indicators (shipments, orders), in-process measures (order error rates), and employee engagement measures (satisfaction, retention, absenteeism) will help us track and course-correct as we implement our changes. As Andrew Atkins and Kevin Cuthbert of Interaction Associates recommend, "What we need to do is move beyond a multi-faceted approach to measurement and take an integrative approach – one that balances multiple dimensions of the business, includes both input and output measures, and most importantly, values qualitative information on a par with quantitative data."[7]

Brotips, a start-up company that posts crowd-sourced quotes with good advice for "bros" – such as "there's a 99% chance that you're awesome, act like it!" – doesn't use the traditional website measure of how many visitors stop at their website. They have more fine-grained measures that tap into the business objectives they are trying to achieve. These include "bounce" (how many people stop at their website but don't stay), number of minutes on their site, and what visitors do at the site, such as post quotes, share tips, or purchase T-shirts with quotes on them.

At a consumer products company, one key measure may be the household penetration of the top brands (as a measure of how many consumers value the benefits those brands offer). Another could be the brand's Net Promoter Score – the number of people who would recommend the brand to a friend. These measures would be part of an integrated scorecard to assess the state of the business.

Many companies focus on too many measures, or they tend to be predominantly activity measures (number of new innovation projects in the pipeline, number of customer calls by sales force) or functional measures (error rate for product supply) instead of including outcome measures. The downside is that we can get lost in a sea of green numbers and ignore the ones that are most important. For example, we've seen products ready to launch with green scorecards on numerous numbers except the big two – meaningful product superiority and strong advertising/media. Without these, the product is unlikely to be successful. We've also seen companies focus on the speed with which a problem is handled rather than whether the customer walked away with a solution.

Lantmännen is an agricultural cooperative owned by 32,000 Swedish farmers, with more than 8,000 employees and operations in over 20 countries. They are the Nordic region's leader in agriculture, machinery, bioenergy, and food products, but not long ago, they faced flat revenues and directionless innovation. So they created an aspirational vision and strategic plan anchored on two key financial targets: 6 percent growth in the core business and 2 percent growth in new organic ventures. These quantitative targets were cascaded down to business units and product groups to foster innovation. Each innovation project group had to demonstrate how the products it was working on would help reach these growth targets for its category and markets. Having clear outcome-focused measures enabled Lantmännen to increase from 4 percent to 13 percent annual growth as a result of the successful launch of a series of new brands. These successes then sparked new growth as innovations were shared and reapplied. Four years after entry into the market, Lantmännen was the market leader in premade food and pioneered a new premium market segment in the industry.[8]

For strategy to succeed, the metrics have to be clear and compelling. They need to measure what matters and enable us to see top-line performance, progress, and results on key indicators in both the short run and the long run. Monitoring these metrics on a regular basis provides the information we need to know to determine whether our strategy still makes sense. It also gives us red flags if we have a winning strategy but our execution is falling flat. Once we see those red flags, quantitative outcomes combined with qualitative data often provide the deep insights that can help us course-correct.

Watch Our Wings

Every good pilot needs a flight plan and working equipment, systems, and crews to get the plane to its destination. But they also need to watch their wings and scan and monitor for the unexpected. The same is true of organizations. We need to anticipate disruptive game changers and monitor our competitive landscape while also keeping an eye on what's happening on the periphery. If we don't, we can be blindsided. As Sergio Marchionne, CEO of Fiat Chrysler Automobiles, said recently, "over the last 10 years we've always had something that came out of left field and made us very, very uncomfortable."[9] For him it was fluctuating oil prices, economic crashes, and currency fluctuations.

Anticipate Game-Changing Forces

External sensing, scanning, and diagnostics involve assessing the surrounding context. Many organizations conduct external diagnostics at the beginning of a change effort and work off forecasting models. Stragility advocates external assessment on an ongoing basis, taking the unpredictability of the future into account. This should include macro-level diagnostics of trends using a tool like PESTE, which analyzes political, economic, social, technological, and ecological forces. It should also entail a competitive analysis of direct competitors as well as those on the periphery (see Stragility Tool 2-2 at the end of this chapter). This means not only taking the time to analyze what has happened and where things are now, but also moving beyond linear forecasting to anticipating and simulating a range of possible disruptive scenarios that may impact our customers and markets, such as digital innovation that makes whole industries obsolete, political upheaval, massive currency fluctuations, global warming, the iCloud, emerging economies, or aging demographics.

A powerful example of a company that missed game-changing forces is Research in Motion, later renamed BlackBerry Ltd. In 2006, BlackBerry was riding high on the wake of mass-market attention and was dubbed the "crackberry" because of its addictive nature in the United States.[10] In 2007, BlackBerry was focused on beating rival Nokia in the cell phone market and was blindsided by the iPhone. At the time, BlackBerry was the dominant keyboard-equipped mobile phone for business use in North America and well known in the global market as well. iPhone came along and disrupted the market, creating essentially a Mac in a cell phone. The iPhone not only appealed to consumers, but it also rapidly stole much of BlackBerry's market share.[11]

To anticipate disruptive forces like these, we need to develop an astute ability to look at our world now and into the future and see ripple effects. The people of Simeulue, also called the "water people" of Indonesia, know how to anticipate and respond to external changes with their fine-tuned skills of reading changes in the sea. The tsunami in Asia in 2004 was one of the deadliest natural disasters in human history, killing over 230,000 people in 14 countries and inundating coastal communities with waves up to 30 meters (100 feet) high.[12]

While dozens of major cities in the region were devastated, nearly everyone on Simeulue survived. Although the last tsunami they saw was in 1907, the Simeulue learn from a young age that if the sea level drops and the water turns "black," they should run for the hills. None of them had experienced a tsunami but their ancestors had, and advice of what to do had been passed on through stories told by the elders. Even children know what to look for. When the tsunami hit in 2004, everyone in that region saw the water recede, but only the Simeulue people looked at it through a different lens and ran for the hills, knowing that this type of "drawback" preceded these seismic sea waves. They lived because they were tuned into and sensed the nuances of changes in water and sand in ways others were unable to perceive.

So what does a story of the tsunami and the people of Simeulue have to do with strategic transformations? Their ability to sense and respond was key to their survival. Similarly, survival in business requires cultivating the skill of sensing and anticipating the key disruptive forces that might matter to us and their ripple effects.[13]

Get Granular

The Stragility approach takes a granular perspective. External conditions, whether macro PESTE forces or competitive forces, affect specific markets, products, regions, and services differently. It is essential that we figure out these impacts and their implications in each market segment or region and continually innovate for new sources of differentiation in our company's product, process, and experiences on a more detailed level.

Tracking best practices, mistakes, and what's happening in the larger landscape can also increase our efficiency, enable us to become a fast follower, and save costly errors. Best practices offer ideas for reapplication and can facilitate our ability to become great fast followers. While first-to-market companies have a high failure rate of 47 percent, fast followers' failure rate is less than 8 percent.[14]

First movers absorb all the start-up costs. Fast followers, in contrast, pick up the already developed idea and focus on refining and scaling it to delight more customers. Did you ever hear of the company Goto.com? Probably not. They showcased their revolutionary search engine in 1998 at a TED conference. Google ran with Goto's ideas, launched in 2000, and now is worth close to $30 billion.[15]

Paying attention to competitors' mistakes can help us avoid similar failures. If it weren't for *E.T.*, the famous movie about an adorable extraterrestrial, the popular Reese's Pieces candy might not exist today. We all remember that heartwarming scene in Spielberg's *E.T.* where Elliott lures E.T. out of hiding using a trail of candy. This trail of Reese's Pieces was originally going to be M&M's, but when the production company approached Mars about using M&M's, Mars said no. After appearing in the film, Reese's Pieces experienced a 65 percent boost in sales, taking market share from M&M's. That scene went down in history as one of the most successful product placements of all time.[16]

Tunnel vision is another weakness that often plagues companies. We're so busy watching one set of trends or competitor moves that we get walloped by something we didn't see. Many of us worry about Ebola and flying in airplanes and pay less attention to everyday killers such as car accidents and heart disease, which are far more likely to kill us.[17] There are a number of books out on cognitive biases such as these, including Dan Ariely's *Predictably Irrational* and Nassim Nicholas Taleb's *Black Swan*.[18] We can prevent some of this blindsiding by watching our wings and continually scanning the periphery for ideas we might reapply.

Finally, we want to be sure that we've done the due diligence for any strategic shift we do choose. That means as we monitor the competitive landscape, we need to watch out for best-practice selection bias. Many executives ask, "Will doing this lead to success?" But equally important questions are "Does *not* doing this lead to failure?" and "Do we have the capabilities to outperform the company we might be fast following?"

Be a Market Maker

Rather than focus on taking share from another competitor, many companies are able to grow by creating new markets. For example, Huggies removed most of the absorbency from diapers to create a new, very profitable category of "swimming diapers."

Snapdeal in India is another great example that illustrates the ability to offer a breakthrough idea by reapplying a first mover's business model but in a new context. Several years ago, Snapdeal was down to its last $100,000 in the bank and nearly out of business. The company was a daily deals retailer in India and business was lower than anticipated. Founder and CEO Kunal Bahl knew he had to shift strategies. This wasn't their first major shift. They had started as a direct marketing company, then moved to online daily deals. Their new aspiration was to become India's online marketplace. Investors were skeptical and many refused to commit new funding. Despite scarce funds, Snapdeal went forward with the new strategy.

The turnaround came in mid-2013, when US-based online marketplace eBay decided to back the company. "It added the necessary validation and credibility to our business," said Bahl. In August that year, eBay and other investors pumped in $50 million. Snapdeal is now on its way to becoming India's hottest marketplace. The company has over 50,000 merchants on its platform, with sales of over $1 billion. And it all happened because Snapdeal was able to "watch its wings": to sense new opportunities and shift strategy to capitalize on them.[19]

Thus, to achieve Stragility and continually win in the market, we need to view external diagnostics as more than examining macro forces at a high level and squeezing out market share from competitors. Instead, external diagnostics become an ongoing, anticipatory, preemptive, fine-grained, mind-opening process along multiple dimensions. The goal of these analyses is to determine what can be learned to help create value over the long run. External diagnostics not only come from the top executives' strategic planning exercises but are also collected and validated by front-liners' "on the beach" observations, by those farther up the hierarchy and by stakeholders and other business partners. These external diagnostics also help us build a compelling case for change, which is essential for creating passion and momentum, a topic that will covered in depth in chapter 4.

Align Internal Capabilities

Sensing, diagnosing, and shifting the internal workings of the organization are also integral to mastering the art of Stragility that will enable winning again and again. To do this, we need to move away from the idea of a static strategic plan. Regular internal checkups and strong ongoing internal diagnostics are critical to ensure that we build on strengths, address pain points, and change the right things.

Leverage Strengths

Too often, we focus exclusively on problems and what's not working. However, identifying what is contributing to the organization's current success is crucial and an often overlooked aspect of Stragility. Understanding what's working well can uncover strengths that should not be disrupted and can also reveal processes or practices in the organization whose broad reapplication might be beneficial. For example, maybe the organization excels at rapid product innovation. While restructuring the organization might appear to be a good solution for addressing new customer opportunities, ensuring that the structural changes being considered do not undermine the rapid communication and decision-making capabilities responsible for the successful product innovation would be equally important.

When Carly Fiorina was head of HP, she and her team studied Bill Hewlett and Dave Packard's original success, values, and approaches and used those learnings to reinvigorate the company and give people confidence that they could do it again. That shared history was both a source of competitive advantage and an immense source of pride for employees.

Evian has also long used its history as a source of competitive advantage and differentiation for both consumers and employees. Legend has it that way back in 1789, a marquis began drinking the water from the Sainte Catherine spring in Evian, France. He claimed it cured him of kidney and liver problems. Today Evian leverages that heritage and talks about their water of "supreme purity" coming from the French Alps.

Toyota leverages their track record of safe, dependable, and affordable cars to grow global market share. This strength has helped them get through recalls quickly and maintain consumer loyalty.

While sometimes leveraging strengths means tapping into history, other times it may entail looking at current innovation, performance, or our customer relationship metrics. To leverage strengths, we need to find pockets of excellence and dig deep to understand why they're doing so well. Asking employees and customers or other stakeholders often reveals capabilities that we don't realize we excel in, which can be re-applied to other divisions or regions of the world (see Stragility Tool 2-4). Identifying what's working well from our stakeholders also provides us with testimonials we can showcase and share to sustain energy and positive buzz – a topic we'll talk more about in the next chapter.

Address Pain Points

Pain points are the symptoms that something is wrong in the organization. They are often complex and hard to fix. Ignoring them won't make them go away. We need to tackle them head on. So, in addition to analyzing what's working well, we need to understand the root causes of things that are not working well. Many times we respond to problems but fail to get to the root causes, so we change the wrong things. Instead, we need to ask what's not working well and then dig for drivers by repeatedly asking "why?" We need to keep peeling back symptoms like layers of an onion to uncover the underlying causes and generate appropriate and effective solutions. Sakichi Toyoda, founder of Toyota Industries in Japan, first applied the notion of the "five why's" in Toyota's manufacturing systems. The five why's is a simple but very effective means of drilling down to root causes.

Take, for example, the story of an organization that had unexpectedly high turnover. In annual surveys, the employees complained about the lack of collaboration and turf wars between departments. To solve that problem, executives in the company decided that a more open physical space would help employees build cross-functional relationships. They spent millions redesigning the office to foster collaboration, only to discover afterward that they needed to dig deeper and ask why again and again. Asking the five why's would have revealed that lack of collaboration and turf wars might be seen as caused by the physical space (first why), different functional specialization (second why), interpersonal difficulties (third why), and/or lack of understanding of strategy (fourth why). Although all of these factors may have contributed to turnover, the fifth why and the underlying root cause of the lack of collaboration between teams was compensation and the bonus systems based on rewarding individual departments. In short, if we don't get to root causes, we run the risk of wasting precious time, money, and effort. We know we've got the root causes when doing the opposite gets rid of the problem. In this case, individual rewards and bonuses became based on the division's ability to deliver product on time and with service excellence, and that solved the problem very effectively (see Stragility Tool 2-4).

Without a clear understanding of the internal diagnostics and drivers, it is impossible to shape solutions that will be successful. Rather than conducting these types of analyses when change is on the horizon, we advocate regular pulse checks and feedback from a multitude of stakeholders to help clarify the drivers on an ongoing basis. We'll discuss this in greater depth in chapter 5, on change fitness.

Shift Strategies and Tactics

As we are redefining or refining our strategic choices, we suggest considering backcasting or best this-day-forward decision-making as possible approaches that might help prevent locking and loading and enable us to better win in the market. First, rather than projecting out scenarios, it's often beneficial to start with where we want to be and backcast to the present. With this lens, we can then figure out what would have to be true to get us to this goal. If sunk costs are holding us back, explicitly ignoring them to make the best this-day-forward decision might be another useful lens to apply.

Backcast the Future

The idea behind backcasting is to envision possible futures the organization or unit aspires to and then work backward to develop the key phases of a story-line that might lead to those visions (see Stragility Tool 2-5). This in is contrast to forecasting, which tends to be based on more linear step-by-step scenarios leading to a future vision. Forecasting also usually starts by trying to solve current problems. With backcasting, we imagine possible future states, then ask ourselves what it would take to get there.[20]

Roger Martin — former dean of the Rotman School of Management, University of Toronto, and author of many books on integrative and design thinking — recommends asking what would have to be true for various options to work. Combining this question with the backcasting lens, we can then determine whether scenarios we're contemplating are realistic. For example, maybe we're assuming but not making explicit that we have to own 80 percent of the market to be profitable on a new initiative. If we've never achieved greater than a 10 percent share on a new product launch, a discussion of what would have to be true might reveal that this expectation is likely unrealistic.

Or imagine we're the CEO of a biotech company and we're trying to figure out the next leading-edge innovation that will disrupt the market for vaccines. We are keen to focus our efforts on immunizations in emerging economies. With a backcasting lens, we ask what would have to be true for us to launch and scale immunizations in developing countries. One factor we uncover is the need for sterilization and refrigeration to keep vaccines safe. That's an important insight uncovered by asking, "What would have to be true?"

But we don't stop there and then try to "forecast" how we could improve refrigeration and provide electricity and sterile conditions in these countries, which might be expensive and time-consuming. Instead of forecasting, we again backcast. We search for different paths that might enable us to achieve our goal. We envision a possible breakthrough future and search for solutions.

Perhaps we discover in tracking industry innovations that Henry Daniell, a biochemistry professor at the University of Pennsylvania, has come up with an idea for cultivating and growing vaccines in the chloroplasts of vegetables.

Hmmm, that holds potential in our minds. This breakthrough idea might lead us to backcasting how to grow the vegetables needed for housing immunizations in emerging economies. Suddenly, we are on to a breakthrough solution of potentially creating vaccines that could be administered orally through vegetables. This would eliminate the costs of immunizations and refrigerated storage needed for current vaccines.

With this example, we see the power of combining asking what would have to be true with backcasting. If we're the CEO of this biotech company, we've uncovered a potential opportunity for launching vaccines that could be more easily scaled.[21]

Backcasting has been used successfully in other fields. Boston Philharmonic Orchestra conductor and professor Benjamin Zander tells the story of how he addressed the grade anxiety of his music students by giving everyone an A at the beginning of the semester and then having them imagine and write about what they did to deserve that A. In effect, he was having them backcast their success rather than anticipate their failure. Letters were written in the past tense as if they had already happened. For example, Giselle Hillyer wrote, "I got my A because I had the courage to examine my fears ... I changed from someone who was scared to make a mistake in case she was noticed to someone who knows that she has a contribution to make to other people, musically and personally ... I have found a desire to convey music to other people, which is stronger than the worries I had about myself."[22] Obviously, the next step for Giselle is to determine what she will have to do to achieve this outcome, such as practice a certain number of hours or increase her number of performances to become more comfortable in front an audience.

Make Best This-Day-Forward Decision

This is another approach to bring to life the Stragility skill of sense and shift. Often companies get locked into ineffective choices due to sunk costs. For example, one study by Hal Arkes and Catherine Blumer asked people to decide whether to invest $1 million in a plane that eluded radar. The results showed that 85 percent of those who were told the project was 90 percent complete would spend the money versus only 17 percent of those who did not know about the sunk costs.[23]

Like these research participants, sometimes if we've already got the patent, built a new line, or have the product on the shelf, we continue throwing good money after bad even if that no longer is a good idea. We should not keep heading in the same direction simply because we have invested heavily in that particular course of action. Instead, we need be willing to cut our losses and shift direction if that makes strategic sense.

Too often, we use language in our deliberations and discussions that exacerbates the sunk-cost effect. We hear people talking about a decision to "stay the course" versus "cut and run." Who would choose the latter option? Cutting losses makes one feel like a coward when the decision is framed in this manner.

Why do we deny, ignore, rationalize, and fail to shift? For most of us, it's hard to admit that we made a wrong decision, or it was a good decision at the time but now it needs revisiting because things have changed. We also don't want to take the blame for "wasting" the time and money already spent. So we keep overly committed to certain activities despite consistently poor results.

Rather than "throwing good money after bad," the Stragility approach advocates creating an atmosphere that values cutting our losses and changing course. Many more top leaders are doing just that. For example, CEO Jeff Immelt has led GE to shift strategy and focus more on their industrial business and less on finance. Sony has done the same thing, shifting out of PCs. Google has what they call moon-shot projects – like driverless cars. Their core business success allows them to place bets on more risky ventures. They do something similar to our risk/cost matrix that we will discuss in chapter 5 and organize investments into short-, medium-, and long-term bets.[24] We need to validate the past and honor our legacy if previous strategies made sense given what was happening then. But we also need to be able to help people in our organization let go of the past and embrace the future if new strategies are needed now.

As leaders in a forever-changing world, we must help our teams consider a variety of different paths for moving forward and cultivate continuous experimentation. We must also be aware of how the seemingly benign micro-practices, such as continually watching our wings or asking "what must be true?" or considering the language used to frame each alternative, can profoundly affect the decisions we make and whether we succeed or fail.

Free the Children: Continuous Transformations to Achieve Purpose and Mission

Free the Children (FTC) is a great example of an organization that has mastered the Stragility principle of continuous strategic sensing and shifting. Free the Children is an innovative, youth-based social-sector organization in Toronto, Canada focused on empowering young people to create social change around the world. FTC empowers youth to take action for change both globally – by building schools, providing clean water, and creating health care centers in poverty-stricken countries including Kenya, Sierra Leone, Ghana, Ecuador, Haiti, Nicaragua, China, and India – and also locally, by creating youth leadership opportunities and tackling social issues that other organizations often walk away from. It is an organization that demonstrates the ability to continuously morph marvelously, and it has helped FTC carve a new path in international charity partnerships and development.

Craig Kielburger was 12 when he founded Free the Children in 1995. He believed that kids could make a difference in addressing educational, health, and poverty issues faced across the world. He fiercely believed that kids – yes, children – could make a difference. They did have a voice and an ability to mobilize others.

The conventional approach to international development when FTC started was adults donating via direct mail, door-to-door canvasing, or telemarketing. Then those charity organizations would go to visible crisis locations, often featured in media, because that helped them raise more money for their cause. NGOs typically competed against each other for scarce funds and deducted administrative expenses from donations.

Introspective from the start and open to wherever the journey might lead, Craig Kielburger and FTC didn't follow the strategic approach of other international development organizations. He literally started tabula rasa with a blank slate, trying different strategies that were consistent with their mission, purpose, and core values. His organization broke all the rules. Even though Craig was told to find some adults who could help him, he decided that FTC was going to leverage the power of kids, not adults.

Today, kids are still the heart of the organization, whether they are running local bake sales, gathering no longer used pennies (in Canada) to the tune of $7 million in a campaign called "Change for Change," building schools in emerging countries, or rolling out initiatives in their schools like Halloween for Hunger or Walk for Water. Not only did FTC shift the engine of the organization from adults to kids, but Craig Kielburger and his brother Mark Kielburger, who joined him as a teen, continuously morphed FTC's strategic approach and business model.

Free the Children's values capture some of this breakthrough thinking: "We live by commitment and passion – WE thinking and WE acting. Getting the job done ... period. Humility, gratitude and appreciation in all endeavors. Honoring every stakeholder. Empowering youth to change the world. Shameless idealism."[25] For every vision generated, they would backcast to what they had now and figure out what they needed to make that vision come alive.

Craig Kielburger's first strategy was to create rescue houses for kids. Then he realized that the children he was trying to help would only stay temporarily and then go back to their villages because they needed to carry water and do chores at home. So FTC shifted their focus to schools and education to break the cycle of poverty. That worked, but then they noticed that girls weren't attending the schools they were building.

So they sensed and shifted again. They created five pillars: Education; Clean Water and Sanitation; Health; Alternative Income and Livelihood; and Agriculture and Food Security. The goal is for each village to never need charity again. Rather than impose Western solutions on these villages as many international development agencies do, they "drink tea" with local villages to learn what their needs are and collaborate with locals to create sustainable success.

Again, breaking with conventional business models and strategic approaches in international development, FTC then branched out to create Me to We. Me to We is a for-profit organization developed "to help transform consumers into socially conscious world changers, one transaction at a time."[26] This sister organization sells ethically manufactured products such as books, clothing, and jewelry and inspiring leadership experiences such as leadership academies and trips to build schools overseas. The profits from Me to We go to supporting FTC, dramatically reducing the need for administrative costs to be deducted from donations and enabling 90 percent of donations to go the cause. Me to We retail products also provide "Track Your Impact" results to show consumers where their purchase made an impact. For example, the purchase of a Me to We backpack might fund education for a child in Sierra Leone for one year. Most recently, rather than compete with other NGOs, FTC is using their annual celebratory We Day in cities across North America as a platform for any social cause. In contrast to the typically competitive model between NGOs, FTC is instead building a cooperative model of partnerships and bridges between charities to tackle the world's most pressing challenges.

Organizations like FTC stay true to their purpose and mission and strategically sense, shift, and transform again and again. They anticipate and sense externally, they learn from competitors' successes and failures, they leverage pockets of excellence, and they backcast for solutions to pain points or to strategically execute breakthrough innovations. Despite skeptics, FTC proved that kids can make a profound difference both globally and locally, that they can build a business model that enables more donation dollars to go to the cause, and that an NGO can be collaborative and succeed by continuously morphing, from the garage of a 12-year-old boy to the international development superstar it is today.

Recap

Sense and shift is a foundational Stragility skill. As we saw with Macy's and P&G, we need to continually fine-tune and revisit our "where to play" and "how to win" choices. We need to ensure everything we do is grounded in our organization's purpose and mission. Unlike BlackBerry, and like the people of Simeulue, we need to watch our wings so we can respond before there's no return. We also need to be market makers like Snapdeal, and we should use the "five why's" to ensure we uncover underlying root causes and don't waste time, energy, and resources on symptoms like the company that poured tons of money into redesigning its physical layout.

When used for developing and redefining strategy, Stragility requires a more fluid and flexible approach to generating ideas that might include backcasting, repeatedly asking what must be true to uncover underlying assumptions, and brainstorming with stakeholders to make best this-day-forward decisions. Meaningful lead measures and metrics will let us know if we are progressing toward our objectives like Brotips and Lantmännen. As we saw with Free the Children, organizations can and must evolve their strategy while maintaining focus on their purpose and mission and adapting to changes in the world around them.

STRAGILITY DIAGNOSTIC TOOL 2-1:
Redefining Strategy to Win: From Lock and Load to Sense and Shift

Stragility Diagnostic				Getting Started
Check the appropriate box: green = good, yellow = needs work, red = major opportunity	Green / Yellow / Red			
Do we have a system for watching our wings for disruptive macro forces?	☐	☐	☐	**Stragility Tool 2-2 Sensing PESTE Forces**
Do we continually monitor our competitive landscape?	☐	☐	☐	**Stragility Tool 2-3 Sensing the Competitive Landscape**
Does our change strategy leverage strengths and address pain points through an understanding of root causes?	☐	☐	☐	**Stragility Tool 2-4 Internal Diagnostics and the Five Why's**
Are we clear on what winning is in our organization and what would have to be true for this change initiative to work?	☐	☐	☐	**Stragility Tool 2-5 Shifting through Backcasting**
Does everyone understand how we will measure success?	☐	☐	☐	**Stragility Tool 2-6 Measuring Success**

STRAGILITY TOOL 2-2:
Sensing PESTE[27] Forces

For each dimension of PESTE, identify key macro forces and their implications for our organization both now and in the future (think nonlinear, disruptive, and discontinuous as well as linear impacts). Which dimensions are key in our industry? What are their implications both now and in the future? What methods do we use to capture and diffuse info?

PESTE Force	Dimensions to Consider	Key Implications
Political (Legal)	e.g., tax policy, employment laws, environmental regulations, trade restrictions and tariffs, political stability, risk of military invasion, intellectual property protection, favored trading partners, antitrust laws, pricing regulations, health and safety regulations	
Economic	e.g., economic growth, interest rates, exchange rates, inflation rates, unemployment levels, discretionary income, infrastructure quality, skill level of workforce, labor costs, business cycle stage (prosperity, recession, recovery)	
Social	e.g., population growth rate, age distribution, social attitudes (health, environmental consciousness, career, etc.), demographics, class structure, education, culture (gender roles, etc.), leisure interests, lifestyle changes, birth and death rates, values/norms/customs	

PESTE Force	Dimensions to Consider	Key Implications
Technological	e.g., rate of technological change, recent technological developments, rate of technological diffusion, new production processes, scientific discoveries, R&D activity, level of automation, government technology incentives	
Ecological	e.g., implications and impact on the planet, community, environment, natural resources	
Other Key Forces and External Stakeholders	e.g., suppliers, distributors, lobby groups, unions, government, community, social-sector organizations	

STRAGILITY TOOL 2-3:
Sensing the Competitive Landscape

List our main competitors across the top row of the grid. Describe their strategy and then assess the strengths and weaknesses of each main competitor in relation to our organization.

Note the potential impact of any indirect competitors and list other key insights about the competitive landscape of our organization (key differentiators, industry success factors, etc.) that it may be helpful to pay attention to for an understanding of our competitive positioning.

	Competitor #1	Competitor #2	Competitor #3	Potential Impact of Indirect Competitors	Other Insights about the Competitive Landscape
Strategy					
Strengths					
Weaknesses					

STRAGILITY TOOL 2-4:
Internal Diagnostics and the Five Why's

What's working well? (place an asterisk after core capabilities, leading practices that are sources of sustainable competitive advantage)

Root Causes? Five Why's?

What things do we not want to change?

What's not working?

Root Causes? Five Why's?

Have we uncovered root causes that if changed would address what's not working?

STRAGILITY TOOL 2-5:
Shifting through Backcasting

- Note insights from external and internal diagnostics
- Imagine best possible alternative futures given diagnostics
- Develop evaluation criteria and ask what must be true
- Assess and converge on best possible future, avoiding sunk costs, and making best this-day-forward decisions
- Pilot and prototype with stakeholders for additional feedback

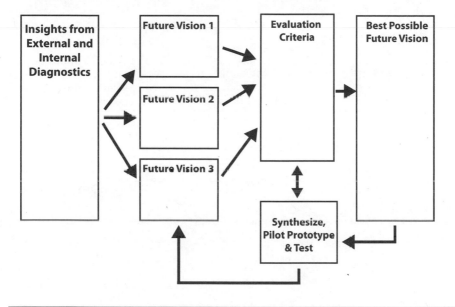

STRAGILITY TOOL 2-6:
Measuring Success

	Quantitative Measures		Qualitative Measures	
	In-process	Outcome	In-process	Outcome
Short run				
Long run				

chapter three

Building Support:
From Poisoned by
the Politics to Embrace
Our Inner Politician[1]

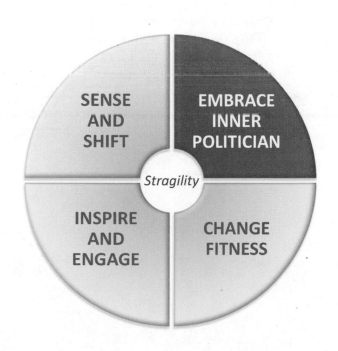

Stragility Skill

Embrace Our Inner Politician

Stragility Success Principles

Develop Political Strategy
- Map political landscape
- Identify key influencers
- Assess influencers' receptiveness to change

Make It Safe
- Leverage pride and historical strengths
- Establish ground rules and create safe language
- Manage emotions explicitly

Cultivate "Better Together" Teams and Solutions
- Face problems together and identify common ground
- Shift focus from yesterday to today and tomorrow
- Be open to fresh ideas

*Unless people are convinced about what you are asking them to do, they
are not going to make it happen. Therefore, one has to keep reasoning
and enable people to come to their own conclusions ... When you are
used to doing things in a certain manner, it takes a long time to orient
yourself to a different way. That's entirely human.*

Ravi Kant[2]

Recall that Stragility involves three elements: strategic, agile, and people-
powered change. In the last chapter, we talked about redefining strategy to
win and staying agile to make course corrections along the way. But that alone
won't enable us to excel at strategic transformation. Even the most brilliant
strategy and the best-laid plans will go up in smoke if we don't address the politics inherent in any change. In this chapter, we walk through another Stragility
skill – how to embrace our inner politician and systematically navigate the
politics and emotions to build support and input for the changes we're lead
ing. In the next chapter, we provide concrete tips and action steps for fostering ownership, commitment, and accountability by inspiring and engaging the
organization as we bring the change to life.

As Carly Fiorina, former HP CEO, said, "A company is a lot like a computer system. Both have purpose or mission. And both have hardware and software. A
company's hardware is its structure, its processes, its plans, its metrics, its results ...
a company's software is its culture of values, habits, mind-sets and behaviors. A
company can't perform better unless both hardware and software are upgraded."[3]

While it is essential to focus on the "hardware" aspects of change – the
strategy, the structure, the metrics, systems, budget, things we often feel we
can control – these factors are typically insufficient for success. We also need
to lead change on the "software" side.

Let's start with politics. Every change has politics as different people jockey
to gain power, make sure they're not losing power, and take sides or positions. Most of us hate the politics because they feel so personally threatening and we feel powerless to deal with them. They're also unpredictable and
can wreak havoc. But ignoring politics and assuming they'll go away is almost
always going to lead to trouble and wasted time, energy, and effort. Innovative
ideas may get suffocated and change goals may be sacrificed for short-term

self-interest. Not only will this change become poisoned, but politics will likely sabotage other changes in the works and set us up for failure for the next change coming down the pike.

In many organizations, talking about politics is taboo. However, not talking about the politics doesn't make political paralysis go away; it leaves everyone scared or furious, poisoning office morale. Backstabbing, blaming, looking back, emotional outbursts, protecting one's own turf to the detriment of the company, and defensiveness are just a few of the behaviors that emerge with political dysfunctions. Although we all worry about politics and how they might derail the changes we're pouring our hearts and energy into, we often feel ill equipped to tackle this area.

Great leaders who are experts at Stragility realize that these seemingly unpredictable aspects of strategic change not only can be navigated effectively, but can even enhance the success of the initiative with the right tools and a systematic approach. So let's see what successfully navigating the politics might look like. We'll start with the story of a new organization leader facing strong opposition, frustration, and his own fears.

KFC: Winning Hearts and Minds

The climate in the room was tense as new KFC president David Novak met with angry franchisees. Their businesses were suffering and they believed KFC's management was not setting them up for success. Many of the franchisees were threatening to leave KFC and go with another restaurant chain.

Corporate/franchisee relations were at an all-time low, with each side blaming the other for lackluster sales and profits. Novak was new to the business, a bit nervous, and not entirely sure how to move forward. He realized that he *and* the franchisees had to get on the same side of the table if they were going to rescue the company. And to do this, both sides had to move beyond focusing on past mistakes and toward a common plan to turn the business around.

He asked everyone what they thought their shared purpose and mission was. He admitted to the mistakes of the past. He heard and acknowledged the frustrations of the franchisees and allowed them to vent and air past grievances. He asked the franchisees about their needs and talked about needs from a corporate point of view. Then he engaged franchisees in creating solutions that would address their common frustrations and pain points.

He started breaking down some of the barriers and was making progress. After initial discussions, he asked the franchisees to pretend they had his job – step into the role of president of KFC – take an hour in small groups, and come back with future priorities. They came back with three: improve quality, launch new products, and train people. And that's exactly what Novak and the franchisees did. "Just like that, we went from 'me' to 'we,'" says Novak. "What ultimately turned KFC around? The finance people will tell you it was the new products we developed ... but I always say it was a triumph of human spirit because we only developed those things once we started working together."[4]

Most of us run away from these types of political minefields that are present in every organization. "Politics" has become a dirty word, rarely discussed and addressed in the workplace. And yet politics are inherent in every change. The KFC story is a wonderful illustration of how to embrace the politics and use them to move change forward. Notice how Novak reminded everyone of their shared mission and purpose, that he admitted mistakes, and finally how he listened, invited input, and then acted on what they developed. These steps laid the groundwork for their eventual turnaround.

In any change we lead, we must focus on the substance of the change *and* the relationship. Emotions run high on all sides. Some people have egos that are easily threatened. Others see only their perceptions and assume negative intent. Some misinterpret what is said. Some form armies of passive resisters if they believe their point of view has been ignored. They say yes but then don't commit. People tend to blame each other when things go wrong. In other words, we're all human with different backgrounds, values, needs, experiences and points of view. By understanding individual and collective stakeholder needs, we'll be more likely to generate creative options that will not only lead to a success on this round of changes but also help create long-run Stragility.

In this chapter, we offer guidance and tips on how to successfully navigate the politics and emotions that are embedded in every change. By proactively mapping the political landscape, creating an environment where it is safe for people to air divergent points of view, and looking for common ground, we can greatly increase our odds of success and build Stragility skills in our organizations for the changes we face now and for the future.

Develop Political Strategy

Many strategic changes derail because, in an effort to circumvent politics, we engage critical players in the organization too late. An important step to attain Stragility is to work with both supporters and skeptics early in the process. That entails mapping the political landscape and developing an engagement strategy, not just for the rollout but throughout the process.

Stakeholder management is certainly not new. Yet most of us launch change by immediately talking with our peers or top management about where the company should go and what changes should be made. While it may be tempting to try to figure out where the company should head with a small group of top executives or those on our team, including key stakeholders from the beginning is crucial for developing the multi-angled input needed for Stragility. Our stakeholders can offer important insights about how the organization is currently performing, external factors that may come into play, and ideas for improvement. Key stakeholder engagement is also critical for ensuring effective implementation as well as cultivating enthusiasm and receptiveness to new initiatives over time.

Map Political Landscape

Like a good politician, we need to start by understanding the political landscape. Mapping the political landscape can be achieved by brainstorming who the key stakeholder groups are and identifying key influencers within those groups. For example, at a large pharmaceutical company, a map of key external stakeholder groups might include different market segments of distributors, customers, suppliers, and government regulatory agencies, as well as lobbying groups and social-sector organizations connected to the firm.

Formal internal groups might be functions, divisions, regions, and levels, but we should also include informal key stakeholder groups and networks such as the longtime employees that eat lunch together every day and the after-work company softball team. It is also useful to differentiate primary stakeholders from secondary stakeholders as we engage in our mapping of the political landscape. Primary stakeholders are those who would be able to offer excellent input to the process and are most directly affected by it. Secondary stakeholders might be able to offer some insight but are less directly affected by the change (see Stragility Tool 3-2).

Identify Key Influencers

Once the important stakeholder groups are mapped, we need to identify the key power players, opinion leaders, or influencers within each group – those individuals who might be able to marshal resources, enroll others, build legitimacy and momentum, and provide ideas crucial to driving the change. These key influencers are those individuals who have the resources, skills, or social networks needed to win over the hearts and minds of the larger group.

Most of us are likely already familiar with the idea of targeting key influencers in external word-of-mouth marketing campaigns. However, we may not have applied that concept internally and thought to identify the key influencers in the changes we lead. These power players are just as critical inside an organization because of their ability to energize or derail change. Influencers can either create a "positive" buzz that helps inspire others in the organization to make changes or, through negative comments, heighten their resistance.

To find key influencers, we should look for those "go-to" people whose opinions can sway others. They might have formal power, such as the top-ranking executive whom many look up to and trust. Or their pull may stem from their expertise, such as an indispensable IT specialist or the creative innovator and problem solver. They might be a central connector creating an information hub within a stakeholder group; or alternatively, they could be a boundary spanner connecting disparate stakeholder groups as part of their role in external relations. It is important to spend time up front identifying these key influencers, listening to their ideas and input, and engaging their participation because they play a critical role in providing resources, enlisting others, and casting the change in a positive or negative light.

This stakeholder mapping should not occur only at the beginning of a change launch. Primary influencers and stakeholders shift as the change evolves, and new people will become critical as the change moves forward. For example,

KFC's franchisees might be critical at every stage of the process, but their ideas about how to provide better service by upgrading the ordering process might require the involvement of the corporate IT group to ensure those changes get worked into the system. It might also be necessary to include legal teams to ensure the changes conform to national and local regulations in the more than 100 countries in which they operate around the world. Then stakeholder mapping might be used in franchisee workforces as franchisee owners implement upgrades in the ordering process locally (see Stragility Tool 3-3).

Assess Influencers' Receptiveness to Change

As we map the political landscape, we also want to begin to assess each group's likely receptiveness to this change and their likely hot-button issues, objections, or fears. And within each group, it is also beneficial to identify the opinion leaders or change agents we hope to get on board.

So how might we think more systematically about politics and receptivity for any particular change initiative? Everyone reacts differently to a change. Some may be eager, enthusiastic, excited, and hopeful. Others may be confused, angry, or uncertain. Everett Rogers's notion of a diffusion curve,[5] later popularized by Malcolm Gladwell in *The Tipping Point*,[6] is often used for analyzing external market segments. The diffusion curve is typically a bell curve, with early adopters at one tail, the majority in the middle, and laggards at the other tail. In our experience, people's receptivity to proposed internal organizational changes tends to follow the same type of diffusion pattern. However, for the purposes of categorizing receptiveness to change, we find it helpful to recast and further divide the diffusion curve from three to six segments: sponsors and promoters, indifferent and cautious fence-sitters, and positive and negative skeptics.

Sponsors and promoters are the most receptive to change. They welcome change and are easily convinced of its merits. Sponsors are particularly helpful for underscoring the benefits to the customer or the organization or for offering resources and lending support. Promoters, in contrast, can create optimistic buzz and help to build passion for and confidence in change. Bringing both of these early adopters on board in the initial phases of change and asking for their support, ideas, input, and commitment can be extremely beneficial in

Table 3.1: Magnet Factors and Action Steps for Sponsors and Promoters

Each sponsor or promoter will have specific reasons, or "magnet factors," that underlie their positive receptivity toward the change. Understanding these magnet factors and developing action steps to cultivate their interest, provide opportunity for input, and enroll them as change leaders can build support and the energy needed for sustaining change.

Sponsors

Potential Magnet Factors	Possible Action Steps
"I believe this change will really benefit the company."	• Ask them to shape and create the plan and the stories that will inspire others to be involved.
	• Enlist them to help lead a visible early win that will reinforce the benefits of the change.
	• Invite them to broadcast the initiative.
"This change is going to help me progress in the company."	• Ask them what they see as the personal and organizational benefits of the change.
	• Give them a role with high visibility and power that will enable them to showcase their successes to the C-suite.

Promoters

Potential Magnet Factors	Possible Action Steps
"I love to be in the know." • Why it's happening • What it is • How it's happening	• Ask their help in framing, developing, contextualizing, and customizing communications – the "why" of change. • Involve them in designing the "what" and the "how."
"I'm excited about working with new people and doing new things."	• Build teams across typical boundaries and be sensitive to creating groups that can work together effectively. • Allow job flexibility and "job swaps" throughout the change to encourage shared learning and broader experience.
"I have great ideas for this change that I'm hoping they'll listen to."	• Solicit early input on content, process, and perceived benefits. • Offer opportunities to lead. Recognize and provide ownership to those who share input and show support.

moving change forward, as they have the power to magnify the positive word of mouth. Table 3.1 offers some typical magnet factors for sponsors and promoters that attract them to change initiatives and some possible action steps to help us build momentum for the change (see also Stragility Tool 3-4).

At the other extreme, influential skeptics tend to fall into two categories. "Positive skeptics" resist a change because they genuinely believe it has flaws that need to be addressed. It is critical that we involve and listen to these folks because they offer a reality check on the proposed changes and implementation. They can be a catalyst for useful rethinking of different aspects and often can help uncover snags and complications that could cause trouble or create backlash.

"Negative skeptics" tend to resist change for more personal and emotional reasons. Often these people are struggling with underlying fears and anxieties about how the change will affect them personally. Working through their concerns is an important part of keeping the change process smooth. Many times, they can be brought on board; they are just at an earlier stage in their transition curve, and once their concerns are discussed they will become more comfortable with the changes in progress. Possible fear factors for positive and negative skeptics and potential action steps are provided in Table 3.2 (see also Stragility Tool 3-4).

In the middle – and in the majority – are the "fence-sitters." They also tend to fall into two groups. The first are cautious fence-sitters. They watch and wait, and are often concerned about the political consequences of moving too fast. They tend to look to their peers for direction or postpone action until most people are on board with change. Indifferent fence-sitters constitute the other category of the middle majority. Their lack of interest might stem from feeling overcommitted or a sense that the change is outside their direct scope of responsibility; or they might also be indifferent because the changes are not integrated directly into their performance metrics. Addressing the concerns of both positive and negative skeptics early in the change process can prevent negative emotions from swaying the cautious or indifferent fence-sitters toward resistance. However, in our experience, it tends to be the energy of influential promoters and sponsors coupled with some early wins that convinces this fence-sitting majority to rally in support of a change.

Rather than guess how receptive folks are about a change, we find it is sometimes better to ask them directly. One approach we use is a tool we call the "passion meter." A passion meter can be as simple as asking people how they feel about the change – "red, yellow, or green light?" For example,

Table 3.2: Fear Factors and Action Steps for Positive and Negative Skeptics

Each positive or negative skeptic will have specific reasons, or "fear factors," that underlie their negative receptivity toward the change. Addressing their concerns, listening to their input, opening up channels of communication, and alleviating their anxiety by taking their fears seriously and developing action steps will aid the change process and minimize the likelihood of resistance.

Positive Skeptics

Potential Fear Factors	Possible Action Steps
"Our team has brilliant ideas for solving these issues, but we're afraid of the consequences if it doesn't exactly work."	Encourage prototyping and learning. Fail fast and cheap, and learn from the experience.
"Nobody talked with us about this. Before this rolls forward, they need to understand all the things that have to be in place for it to work here."	Preemptively gather input and ideas on how to integrate new changes. Enroll a rep from this stakeholder group so that they can shape the "what" and the "how" from the start.
"This change is too risky and too costly."	Explore whether there are ways to minimize risk and reduce cost. Demonstrate long-run benefits associated with the change.

Negative Skeptics

Potential Fear Factors	Possible Action Steps
"I've worked hard to get where I am, and this change is going to mess it all up."	Dig deeper on what they think is going to be messed up – important insights for the "what" and "how." Customize to underscore meaningful benefits for them and provide the training needed. Be open and transparent about any serious uncertainties.
"I don't understand this change." • Why it's happening • What it is • How it's happening	Take the time to ask for input and perceptions of impact on the "why," "what," and "how." Develop stories that create an emotional connection to which they can relate. Let them shape the process.
"It's hard to make change work here. What makes this one any different?"	Disassociate this change with previous changes by emphasizing differences in who's leading the change, the content, and the process. Build multi-stakeholder teams to provide input into and lead change.

at one large global Fortune 500 company, "coffee connects" were conducted to gauge people's reactions and gather feedback on an upcoming strategic change initiative. During these conversations, employees were asked whether they were ready to give the "green light" on a change, felt the need to slow down, or wanted the company to stop and take a step back. Beyond gauging employees' level of enthusiasm, the passion meter's more important purpose is to enable change leaders to probe and learn why people feel the way they do (see Stragility Tool 3-2).

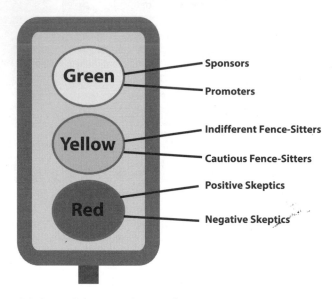

Figure 3.1: Receptiveness to Change: The Passion Meter

We should also note that for a change to work, we *don't* have to have everyone on board. But we do need to have critical mass. We also must keep in mind that one explosive outbreak can open up an opportunity for engagement and improvement, as CEO David Novak learned from his KFC franchisees. Or it can derail the entire process, as Hostess, the maker of Twinkies, discovered when they didn't move quickly enough to manage the politics brewing in that organization. Management and the union failed to reach an agreement and the business was shut down.

Make It Safe

Identifying different reactions to change and preemptively managing with action steps are both crucial. Another key factor is whether people feel safe and comfortable expressing their thoughts and emotions. Often change derails because people never really understand each other's points of view. Higher levels or change leaders just tell and sell their position and wonder why nothing happens. Lower levels tell us what they think we want to hear, without highlighting difficult on-the-ground realities. No one probes for the reasons people are feeling the way they are, frustrations mount, and emotions explode, derailing interventions that may have helped solve the issues.

Often senior management is shielded from the on-the-ground realities by well-intentioned leaders eager to sell the change. Even when they face resistance, they plow forward. The recent sit-in at Colgate University is a great example of how both students and the administration created a safe environment to discuss a hot-button issue and agree on a plan to make radical changes (see Stragility Tool 3-4).

Colgate University: Turning Protest into Passion for Joint Action

The week did not start out well for Colgate University president Jeffrey Herbst. At 8:15 Monday morning, more than 300 students staged a sit-in at the university's admissions building to protest the treatment of minority students on campus. The problem had been simmering for some time and the mood was angry and tense. The students publicized the effort on social media using the hashtag #CanYouHearUsNow and posted video testimonials of racist incidents.

Surprising many in the room, the student leaders presented the president with their demands in a non-threatening way with a focus on common ground. They first stated how deeply they believed in Colgate's mission as an inclusive learning institution. They acknowledged that the problem was one of the most difficult faced by all institutions in the United States and globally. With achieving Colgate's mission as their goal, they listed their concerns and action plans.

Instead of reacting defensively, calling police, or otherwise escalating the situation, Herbst and other university leaders sat with the students and listened to their stories.

Students spoke in raw, emotional terms about greatly painful experiences that stemmed from issues of race and identity, as well as class, sexual orientation, and, for international students, national origin. They recounted occasions when they had been insulted on campus, felt marginalized both inside and outside of the classroom and felt unsafe. Many were moved to tears by their heart-wrenching stories.[7]

This honest, open sharing set the stage for both sides to understand each other and find agreement. The students acknowledged that this problem was not unique to Colgate. The administration showed its strong support for their efforts and positive approach to solving the issues.

Herbst realized that the university and the students were unified in their desire for a resolution. He condemned the racist incidents and expressed his and the university's solidarity with the students taking part in the sit-in. As he said in an email to alumni midweek,

As you may have heard, there is an ongoing peaceful demonstration on Colgate's campus in support of inclusion and diversity. We have made significant progress toward mutual understanding regarding a 21-point list of "concerns and action plans" that were submitted to us by the student organization, Colgate University Association of Critical Collegians (ACC). Over the past two days, we have met for many hours with ACC representatives to discuss their concerns. We also joined the sit-in to listen to the students' stories of having endured incidents of racism, classism, homophobia, and sexism on campus ... We have heard our students and community members, and we join with them in the common goal of creating a campus environment that is welcoming and supportive of all.

Note the inclusive language he uses: "peaceful demonstration ... mutual understanding ... joined the sit-in ... common goals." The sit-in lasted almost a week, during which all sides made significant progress in understanding the issues and developing an action plan. The students made a list of 21 demands. The university listened and *together* they formulated a joint plan to address the issue. That Friday, Herbst said in a statement,

The peaceful demonstration in support of inclusivity on Colgate's campus has come to a mutually agreeable resolution, as members of the administration and the Colgate University Association for Critical Collegians (ACC) released a 21-point road map for the future ... As a liberal arts institution, we must do everything we can, together, to create an environment that is welcoming to all students, so that all can freely explore diverse perspectives and worldviews.

ACC founders said, "Colgate must fulfill its promise of being an inclusive institution for students of all backgrounds. Our hope moving forward is that this new action plan will create lasting change in our campus community."

This story is a great example of making it safe to air differences, facing the problem versus facing off against each other, being inclusive, really listening, and identifying common needs and solutions to create lasting change. The key principles the leaders employed of leading proactively with a strong purpose, values, principles, and a track record of valuing people's input, high trust, and high accountability enabled this conflict to be transformed into a mutual commitment toward a new and better future.

So how can we create un-siloed, accountable organizations? We can start by soliciting feedback directly from lower levels of the organization, not filtered through a chain of command. Yes, talking directly to the front line might seem time-consuming, but not compared to the time spent trying to undo resistance to change. Unless we give people permission, they will not be able to share controversial feedback, which may be our early warning signal that something is going wrong. We also need to follow up and probe for why people are feeling the way they are. For example, a solution that looks good from the top may not actually solve a pain point of those tasked with executing it. Or maybe a fear of job loss is creating resistance. By learning from all types of people, from early adopters to skeptics to naysayers, we can preemptively prevent politics from escalating out of control. Simple tactics such as giving credit for ideas and identifying great builds that are "their idea" go a long way. We can also directly ask skeptics what would have to be true for them to endorse the change.

Leverage Pride and Historical Strengths

Often the values, strategy, and culture that made the firm successful in the first place can help support the new change. Indeed, McKinsey & Company found that organizations that understood and built on strengths when planning transformation were twice as likely to succeed than those that focused primarily on problems.[8]

CEO Frederic Rose confronted this dilemma of maintaining company strengths while leading a major downsizing of Technicolor SA. Technicolor SA is a multi-billion-dollar company with headquarters in Issy-les-Moulineaux,

France, that provides services and products for the communication, media, and entertainment industries. He had to keep the company's innovation expertise alive through the tough times. To do this, he was careful to preserve R&D investments and anchor them as the center of the company's turnaround.

As Rose shared in an interview, "It was 2008, the company was flooded with debt and struggling to prepare for the transition from analog to digital. When we were at low tide, people said 'You need to cut your investment costs,' and I thought, 'OK, but if we do that and we don't drown, what do we do in five years?'" Rose told *Variety*, "My nightmare was to wake up out of this entire turnaround venture and realize that the bankers were happy but we had really nothing left."

In order to get Technicolor back in the black, Rose says, he was forced to "spend a lot of time rethinking our entire workflow process and find ways to use more of our assets ... If you want to stay relevant you have to constantly rebuild yourself, retool, re-upscale yourself and you can only do it by training your people and bringing new people in. If you don't do it, you end up with groupthink, and that's when things go to hell."

Rose's strategic plan reduced Technicolor's debt while maintaining its investment in technical innovation – its historic pillar of success. Today, the company holds more than 40,000 patents and creates about 2,000 new ones every year. By building on their innovation strength to make changes, they saved the company and set it up for future success.[9]

In contrast, consider the example of railroading a change and creating a poisonous political atmosphere that occurred at one major global bank. The CEO "Jack Frost" (not his real name) had a reputation for being the iceman. People feared his wrath and stopped sharing ideas. The bank endured a major slump when it missed major market shifts. This CEO tried to turn things around. But he did so by force-feeding a major technology change from the top, with no training or backup for the new system and unrealistic timelines. He made the numbers but at a huge political and emotional cost to the organization. They lost high performers, alienated the front line, triggered union picketing, and tarnished their reputation in the market when they failed to file Federal Reserve reports and "lost" customers' account information. The trauma of that turnaround still haunts the organization. The next CEO spent months investing in establishing trust and building relationships to overcome the dysfunctional political quagmire she inherited.

Now consider BlackRock, a company that has emerged as one of the key players in the investment management industry because of its ability to attract and retain top talent. BlackRock credits their strong culture for becoming the largest asset management firm in the world, with assets of $3.3 trillion. From the CEO to the front line, they talk about One BlackRock, which is purpose driven, performance oriented, and principles led. And they live it. At BlackRock, everyone has a voice. Their values reflect their commitment to full engagement from their employees. "Be respectfully anti-bureaucratic, challenge the status quo, and don't be afraid of failure."[10]

Establish Ground Rules and Create Safe Language

By establishing ground rules and then modeling them in our own behaviors, we find we get much more honest and valuable input. In one change effort, we (the authors) worked on, ground rules generated by the team included the following: be the change (role model the desired new behaviors yourself), go slow to go fast (e.g., take time to build relationships and understanding), and assume positive intent (believe that everyone is prioritizing the group's and the company's best interests). These ground rules dramatically and positively affected how different, previously clashing divisions communicated with each other. We all have fragile egos and strongly held positions and easily become defensive when threatened. We found that changing the way ideas and feelings are communicated enabled greater understanding while lowering defensiveness.

We also developed safe language to express feelings. Often the language we use gets in the way of understanding and creating better solutions. Using the approach of the leadership training company MatrixWorks, founded by Mukara Meredith, we adopted new language. Instead of talking about likes and dislikes, we talked about likes and "wish for's," and we learned to say "yes and" rather than "no" or "but." When something didn't feel right to someone they'd talk about their "inner squeeze." If someone's attention seemed to be wandering, we would ask if they were "in" (fully present) or "out." When things got tough and we failed to agree, we reminded ourselves of these ground rules. Other great ones we have used are "don't worry, don't hurry," "trust the process," and "lean into chaos."

Manage Emotions Explicitly

When we are tired, overwhelmed, multitasking, and bouncing from one thing to the next, we all have a shorter fuse. As effective change leaders building Stragility in our organizations, we need to develop skills for recharging ourselves (which we'll discuss in chapter 5) and for working with people who are emotionally spent.

One thing we can do when working with those who are emotionally resisting change is give them a chance to vent. It's often very important to let people share their frustrations and feel heard. By listening empathetically, putting ourselves in their shoes, and validating their point of view, we show our compassion. In the process, we also often learn useful tips about roadblocks, better ways of doing things, and what's really going on in our team's minds. As we listen, we want to try to provide insight and feedback to address skeptics' concerns, but we do not want to assume that we understand all the underlying motivations for someone's behavior. We see what their fears are, validate that they are being heard, and see how we can move forward. We also use "We/I vs. You" language and avoid blaming language. For example, we wouldn't say, "The reason this change is needed is that your team isn't performing up to par." Instead, we'd reframe with this: "How can we work together to better launch this change and meet our goals for this division?"

It also can be beneficial to talk about our emotions: "I'm feeling let down" versus "you didn't do what you said you would," or "I'm feeling nervous and frustrated because ..." We (the authors) worked with a small multifunctional team that was tasked with creating one unified organization across previously siloed divisions. We interviewed the core team individually before the first meeting to understand each person's wishes, concerns, and fears. From these interviews, we realized there was a lot of fear of losing what was special about each function. People also lacked knowledge about what the other functions really did. Based on this background information, we organized a week-long offsite session both to craft a common vision for the new organization and to build relationships and trust among the core team. This investment in time and relationships proved to be the foundation for creating and maintaining the new organization.

As the new combined organization came together, we began meetings with a pulse check on how people were feeling, using the idea of green, yellow, or red lights that we mentioned earlier in this chapter. However, this time, we took it one step further and had people report on their head, heart, and hands. For example, one woman said she was "let's go" green on head (fully on board with the new solution), and she was green on heart (feeling great emotionally about the new possibilities), but red on hands – she simply didn't have the staff to pull off all that we had committed to in her department. By understanding all three dimensions, we were able to assess where things were off track and address the staffing squeeze by phasing the work and stopping some things that were taking staff time but no longer really needed.

We often found that people shared what was happening to them outside of work. This helped the group understand each person more holistically and helped us support each other as full people – not just as work selves. Admittedly, these check-ins took time and there were days when we were impatient to move through the agenda more quickly. In most cases, however, really knowing what was happening with one another reinforced their commitment to the project, trust in each other, and belief that they could be their whole selves at work.

Another organization faced the difficult change challenge of closing a plant. It was during the global financial crash, and Isaac (as we'll call him) was managing a plant that corporate had decided needed to be shut down as customer demand plummeted. Operations were going to be centralized in another country. Despite customer demand dropping, the plant had to fulfill over $30 million in orders before closing, and it needed the skills and capabilities of the workforce to transition effectively. Other companies' plant closures in the region had resulted in protests and violence, so many companies were not telling their employees if they were shutting down until the last minute.

Isaac was nervous about taking on this role but decided that honesty and empathetic engagement would be the key values he would lead with. He told employees that the plant was closing nine months in advance and shared his own fears openly. Isaac spent 60 percent of his time managing emotions, providing support, and working with his employees to help them find new jobs. Isaac's authenticity and willingness to work through personal issues led to success. The plant remained open long enough to fulfill customer orders, and employees helped transition the centralized team into their new roles. This plant was one of the few that closed without violence or lockouts.[11]

As we see in all these examples, as change leaders, we can make it safe for those who will help with the transition by leveraging pride and historical strengths as at Colgate or Technicolor SA, establishing ground rules and creating safe language as we did with the organization we led a week-long retreat with, and managing emotions explicitly even when facing a plant closure.

Cultivate "Better Together" Teams and Solutions

One team we (the authors) worked with had a theme song – "Better When We're Together" by Jack Johnson – as their inspiration. And that's certainly the spirit we find when we can come together to achieve our goals. The diversity of the team, which caused the initial friction, became an advantage once trust was built.

Our goal in any change is to get all parties on the same side of the table and future-focused, finding ways to drive the change toward the desired outcomes, rather than on different sides arguing their positions or rehashing past grievances. There are some political tactics that can help. One is finding common ground that transcends differences. A second is inviting people to participate, which both gives them a stake and enables the gathering of ideas from broader stakeholders. A third is to agree on the process even if we can't agree on outcomes or goals quite yet. A fourth is to provide listening and cooling-off time before trying to proceed on goals and specifics. As former South African president Nelson Mandela noted, "If you want to make peace with your enemy, you have to work with your enemy. Then he becomes your partner."[12]

Face Problems Together and Identify Common Ground

At a company we'll call KLS in Latin America, Lucia Martinez (not her real name) found common ground. Having stepped into the position of CEO six months earlier, taking over the post from retiring CEO Pablo Garcia (not his real name), she knew now was the time to start taking action. She admired and respected Pablo greatly. Pablo had been a wonderful mentor. Yet she also knew it was essential for the company to regain its competitive edge and position itself for the future. Global competition and the fluctuating value of the dollar as well as a myriad of other external pressures were taking their toll. Over the prior two years, KLS Corporation saw eroding market share and increasing customer complaints, and they were slow to get new customers.

While some within the company were anticipating and even anxious to see what Lucia would do, others were much more reluctant. They liked the way things were and still were not used to her as CEO. As she thought about the company, she mulled over some of the issues she knew she had to address. One persistent problem was the constant battles between various functional areas and the incredible fiefdoms that had built up. The good news was that most people in the organization were very loyal to their divisions.

The bad news was that the battles between departments tended to escalate and took so much time and energy that company objectives often got lost in the shuffle. Product development complained they never got feedback from the customer through sales or marketing. Sales complained production never manufactured the product cheaply enough to compete. Manufacturing complained product development gave them designs that could not be mass-produced. Meanwhile, sales gave away products with no concern for margin. Market research argued that they collected great data that no one ever took seriously or acted on, so customer responsiveness was a joke.

The same battles happened again and again. Somehow, the focus had to shift from what was good for my department to what was good for the company and the customer, but it was going to be an uphill climb. Significant changes would be required to break down these long-established turf wars and mindsets.

Lucia had the sense people throughout the organization were putting in time but not their hearts or their ideas into the company. What could she do to change that? There were many talented and high-potential people in this organization; she just had to figure out how to better tap those capabilities and make the company more than, instead of less than, the sum of its parts.

The first thing Lucia did was align everyone on vision. Although each of the functional departments had issues with the others, they all were upset by the recent downturn in KLS's results and shared a common dream of wanting KLS to again become a star in the industry. To reinforce that common ground, Lucia instituted an annual profit-sharing bonus that provided incentives for departments to work together. The more the company sold, the bigger the bonus for everyone. Next, she created cross-functional teams to conduct diagnostics and generate solutions for various pressing issues the company faced. This forced each individual to begin to think about things from the perspective of the other departments and what was good for the company. When it came to implementation – including concrete actions, responsibilities, next steps, and how the changes would be monitored – she created a cross-functional multi-level task force to lead and manage the process. By breaking down barriers and unifying everyone behind a common vision, she turned the company around and built pride, momentum, and energy across the organization, which have carried the company through subsequent challenges.

Shift Focus from Yesterday to Today and Tomorrow

The more people feel that their point of view is heard, see some of it reflected, and know that they helped create the solution, the more likely they'll become promoters. The added benefit is that these early adopters will begin moving themselves and their organizations toward the new behaviors, so the learning curve when the change is implemented will be less steep.

Often, we are leading or implementing change efforts to turn around results. Michael Kaiser is known as the arts organization "turnaround king" because of his many successful turnarounds in the arts industry, from Alvin Ailey to the United Kingdom's Royal Opera House to the Kennedy Center. According to Kaiser, "troubled arts organizations are angry, sad and defeated ... the entire organization focuses on the size of the problem, the cause of the problem, and whom to blame ... a great deal of effort is spent looking backward ... and there's lots of infighting."[13]

> Turnarounds take a huge investment in energy, emotion, and time. They are also incredibly scary. While it is fun and gratifying, in retrospect, to look at the steps one took to solve serious problems, when one is in the initial stages, it is very frightening ... One comes to work each day not certain whether one has the funds to survive until the next day ... The staff and artists are demoralized by the anger they encounter from vendors, by the lack of resources, and by fear and exhaustion and uncertainty. They are in great need of leadership and support and encouragement.[14]

As with our Stragility approach, Kaiser suggests that we build support for change by engaging key influencers and gathering their points of view of how to move forward. For example, when he was brought in to help Alvin Ailey, the largest modern dance ensemble in the world, the company was deeply in debt and their survival was in jeopardy. His first step was to develop a strong relationship with the artistic director and reassure her that they would partner to achieve her vision for the troupe. Without her leadership and a strong creative product, there would be no turnaround. To galvanize the board, they held a full-day retreat to craft a new mission and plan. Their plan focused on marketing and fundraising with a mantra of "Good art, well marketed" to appeal to both audiences and patrons. And it came to life via a series of successful events, from performing at President Clinton's Inaugural Ball, a free Central Park performance, a Smithsonian exhibit, and great new programming. Each of these events was meaningful. Taken as a group, they "redefined the Ailey Company as the hottest and sexiest dance organization of the time."[15] The organization doubled its fundraising, got its finances in order, and created multi-year programming that brought it years of future success.

As Kaiser notes, turnarounds are hard on leaders. He reports being greeted by nasty letters and pitying glances from nearly everyone. But when one change effort succeeds, it unleashes the organization's energy and builds momentum. "The power and energy and excitement when a troubled arts organization truly turns the corner and can look to the future rather than dwell on the past creates as intensely satisfying a moment as I have experienced."[16]

Be Open to Fresh Ideas

Beyond shifting from divisive teams to stronger collaboration by finding common ground and focusing on the future rather than the past, like Lucia Martinez at KLS, we also want to actively engage stakeholders about their ideas for what to do and how. There is never just one way to do something or just one option. By enrolling key stakeholders in creating the solutions, we can discover new paths for eliminating roadblocks and barriers. For example, in one major restructuring, people were resisting change for fear their ratings would drop as they took on new jobs and learned new skills. To counter this fear, management agreed to freeze ratings for that first transitional year. Often, rather than letting frustrations escalate, we can open up new avenues and solutions by explicitly asking what new ideas those concerned have for addressing their issues.

When doing this, we often find that it helps *not* to have senior management in the room initially. We might empower a key influencer to become a facilitator, bring together those who have concerns, and ask them to create flip charts with what challenges they face with their teams. We might then train them on the five why's for finding root causes, as discussed in chapter 2. From there, we might brainstorm on backcasting alternative breakthrough solutions. Then we might invite senior management back in the room to look for points of convergence and to discuss the flip charts and options with the teams. We find that sometimes creating a more anonymous forum for airing concerns and recommendations preempts paralyzing resistance. It also reduces people's anxieties and enables them to generate more robust stakeholder inclusive action steps. The combination of input from those most affected, their ownership of solutions, and our openness to better approaches accelerates adoption in unimaginable ways.

Michael Abrashoff, former captain of the USS *Benfold* (a 9,000-ton naval destroyer), tells the story of a great time- and money-saving idea that came from a young enlisted sailor who hated all the hours and days his crew had to spend painting the ship six times a year. This was standard practice on every ship in the US Navy. The painting was necessary to cover up rust streaks that occurred at every place metal was fastened together. The sailor suggested replacing the fasteners with no-rust stainless steel. With that small change they could go two years between paintings, freeing the crew up to do more meaningful work. That one idea was adopted by the entire US Navy, saving countless hours and money.[17]

Samsø: Embracing Change to Create a Renewable Energy Community

As the English poet John Donne famously said in the late 1500s, "No man is an island." In our next story, we'll learn how even people who live on islands must navigate politics to get anything done. Samsø, a small Danish island about four hours from Copenhagen, has become a global model for how communities can become greener. Over a 10-year period, the island has moved from a dependence on expensive fuels to the world's first 100 percent renewable-energy-powered island. It is change journey that illustrates a number of the success principles embodied by the Stragility skill of embracing our inner politician.

Søren Hermansen and his wife Malene Lunden have led the project since inception, but they didn't do it alone. Hermansen realized the project's success would ultimately be driven by the politics of the community and whether they could persuade widely different groups of people that the project was in their own best interest.

As he said in a 2015 interview, the key barrier is people's fears. "So many projects run into really big problems because people get afraid of the changes. They fear the consequences of the changes more than they like the potential benefits. I have seen this so much that I knew it was time to address this conflict and find a way to overcome it. People feel much more interested in the project if they are a part of it, if they have invested part of their savings in it."[18]

He first identified different key stakeholder groups – farmers, government, residents, summer home owners – and what he called the "blacksmiths" in each group.[19] These are the people capable of bending steel to get things done – what we'd call the promoters and sponsors.

Then he and his wife Malene began a seemingly endless series of meetings over coffee and beers to understand the needs of each group and appeal to their direct and practical self-interest. The appeal had to include concrete benefits like more income, cheaper fuel, and cleaner water for their children to drink rather than vague, altruistic, "it's better for the planet" claims. For example, plumbers were worried they would lose business as people got rid of oil burners. Hermansen took them for beers and explained that they could get more business by servicing the new heat pumps. Farmers dismissed it as a "hippie project" dreamed up in Copenhagen with no benefit for them. A team of early adopter farmers created a new revenue stream from cultivating elephant grass as a source of biomass for heating plants. Residents were helped with applying for grants to update old houses. Even the golf course got into the action. They now use sheep to mow the greens (yes, we said "sheep mow the greens!") and give members hand weeders to help control weeds as they play.[20]

As Hermansen mentions in his TEDx talk, this isn't a technology success story so much as it is a lesson in the large-scale transformations that are possible when you engage people.[21] Ultimately, all successful change projects are people-powered. It entails identifying the stakeholders and adoption groups, inviting participation, understanding their needs and fears, finding common interests, and delivering benefits to each group. Hermansen is now director of the Samsø Energy Academy, helping other communities become greener by embracing their inner politician and gaining widespread public participation and passion for the change.

Recap

To ensure success, we know we must not only address the mechanics of change; we must also systematically work with the very real political and emotional dynamics in change, as these forces can either thwart the best-laid plans or be a source of energy and momentum. When we do this well, we can transform the anger, sadness, and defeated feelings that Michael Kaiser speaks of in the Alvin Ailey story into our own versions of "the hottest and sexiest dance organization of the time."

In addition, we need to continually stay on top of these dynamics, because the political and emotional landscape will shift for each change initiative we lead and will evolve over time, as we saw with David Novak's story of KFC's turnaround. Early reactions may swing in the opposite direction once people become engaged in the unfolding change process, as momentum builds and as the personal and organizational outcomes become known. Similarly, a sponsor for one initiative may be a negative skeptic on another.

Taking the time to identify influential people and enable them to share their enthusiasm and propel change forward, as well as working with those more reticent about change to understand their concerns, gather their ideas, and gain their commitment, is critical. We saw the power of influencers in virtually all of our stories in this chapter. And offering a benefit for each group, as in the Danish island example, is key.

In addition, we must make it comfortable for people to share their views, leverage pride in the company, and establish ground rules and safe language. Once everyone feels like they can voice their ideas, we have the ideal foundation to be a better, stronger organization together. Colgate University's sit-in and the resulting joint action plan is a great example of doing this well, as is our story of Samsø in Denmark. We can identify the common ground we all share and more easily shift our focus from past grievances to future solutions, all while being open to fresh ideas that emerge along the way.

We bet your people have ideas they are eager to share, like rustless fasteners that eliminated frequent ship repainting. Who knows what simple breakthrough ideas might emerge if we embrace our inner politician and invite our stakeholders to join us. Particularly now when change is ubiquitous and each change dovetails and overlaps with others on the horizon, honing the Stragility skill of embracing our inner politician is more important than ever.

STRAGILITY DIAGNOSTIC TOOL 3-1:
Building Support: From Poisoned by the Politics to Embrace Our Inner Politician

Stragility Diagnostic	Green / Yellow / Red	Getting Started
Check the appropriate box: green = good, yellow = needs work, red = major opportunity		
Have we mapped the key stakeholders for this change?	☐ ☐ ☐	**Stragility Tool 3-2 Stakeholder Mapping**
Have we identified the key influencers and their receptivity? Do we know our sponsors, promoters, fence-sitters, and positive and negative skeptics?	☐ ☐ ☐	**Stragility Tool 3-3 Key Influencer Identification and Receptivity Mapping**
Are we clear on magnet factors and fear factors by stakeholder group and for our key influencers?	☐ ☐ ☐	**Stragility Tool 3-4 Stakeholder Engagement**
Do we have an engagement plan for engaging sponsors and promoters, fence-sitters, and positive and negative skeptics?	☐ ☐ ☐	**Stragility Tool 3-4 Stakeholder Engagement Also see Table 3.1 and Table 3.2**
Are we leveraging pride, developing safe language (e.g., likes and "wish for's," "yes and"), and establishing ground rules (e.g., assume positive intent, be the change) to increase likelihood that alternative points of view will be heard and new ideas incorporated?	☐ ☐ ☐	**Stragility Tool 3-4 Stakeholder Engagement Also see Table 3.1 and Table 3.2**
Do we have open communication channels to enable us to find common ground, gather fresh ideas, and manage emotions explicitly?	☐ ☐ ☐	**Stragility Tool 3-4 Stakeholder Engagement**

STRAGILITY TOOL 3-2:
Stakeholder Mapping

Map the key stakeholder groups. List the key stakeholder groups (internal, external, formal, and informal) that will be impacted by this initiative. Asterisk the **primary** stakeholders (those directly affected by the change) to distinguish them from the **secondary** stakeholders.

	Formal	Informal
External		
Internal		

STRAGILITY TOOL 3-3:
Key Influencer Identification and Receptivity Mapping

Place each primary stakeholder group within a circle.

Identify key influencers within each stakeholder group. Write their initials/names in the box attached to the relevant circle.

Assess change receptivity using the passion meter for each key influencer. Denote with green (sponsors and promoters), yellow (cautious and indifferent fence-sitters), or red (positive or negative skeptics) for each and note why.

Revisit as the politics shift over time.

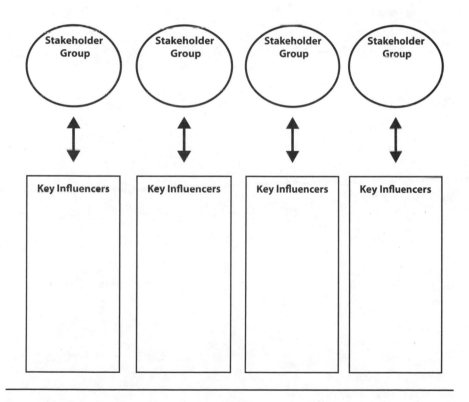

STRAGILITY TOOL 3-4:
Stakeholder Engagement

Revisit key stakeholders and influencers in each category (sponsors, promoters, cautious and indifferent fence-sitters, positive skeptics, negative skeptics) and remap as needed.

Generate action steps for each based on their magnet factors and fear factors (see Table 3.2).

Develop safe language (e.g., likes and "wish for's," "yes and") and establish ground rules (e.g., assume positive intent, be truth tellers) to increase likelihood that alternative points of view will be heard and incorporated.

Keep communication channels open for input, emotions, and fresh ideas.

	Who	Action Steps
Mobilizing Sponsors		
Mobilizing Promoters		
Engaging Fence-sitters		
Learning from Positive Skeptics		
Addressing Concerns and Fears of Negative Skeptics		

Fostering Ownership
and Accountability:
From Tell and Sell to
Inspire and Engage

At a Glance: Fostering Ownership and Accountability

Stragility Skill

Inspire and Engage

Stragility Success Principles

Ignite Passion through the "Why?"
- Share the vision and business case
- Connect with story
- Create a mantra

Go Slow to Go Fast
- Let go of the past
- Provide the resources, skills, and training needed
- Communicate, communicate, communicate

Stay Close to the Action
- Distribute ownership and accountability
- Offer help and hope

How strange that the nature of life is change, yet the nature of human beings is to resist change. And how ironic that the difficult times we fear might ruin us are the very ones that can break us open and help us blossom into who we were meant to be.

Elizabeth Lesser[1]

Change is disturbing when it is done to us, exhilarating when it is done by us.

Rosabeth Moss Kanter[2]

In the last chapter, we walked through the Stragility skill of embracing our inner politician to systematically navigate the politics and the emotions and build receptivity to the changes we're launching and leading. In this chapter, we explore another skill essential for Stragility. We provide success principles, concrete tips, and action steps for building on the support and momentum gained, by moving from receptivity to inspiring and engaging those in the organization to take action.

All change starts with us – with one person taking action, then another, then another. Done right, Stragility unleashes the power of people to make change happen. Most of us don't do a very good job of inspiring and engaging the people in our organizations. We tell and we sell the change or we under-communicate and assume they understand. We give them the big picture but fail to translate that into what it means for them in their daily work. We force-feed and push. And then we're surprised when even a change that will clearly benefit them is resisted, when people are cynical, when they seem to check out or actively sabotage the effort.

Well, maybe we shouldn't be so taken aback. Although well intended, the "tell and sell" approach rarely leads to the change outcomes we seek. We may get activity, but we likely won't get the necessary buy-in and engagement. People won't be able to work through the pain that's part of every change to realize the gains both for the organization and for them personally. Disengagement plagues most companies, whether they are in the midst of change or not. Indeed, a Towers Watson global workforce study of 32,000 employees in medium and large companies in 29 countries showed that only 21 percent of employees were fully engaged at work and a full 40 percent were disengaged.[3] These numbers likely get worse during transformations and turnarounds if efforts are not made to truly inspire and engage.

John Pepper, former chairman of the board of Disney and former chairman and CEO of P&G, describes it this way:

> Accountability and ownership for people will not come as a result of a command; they flow from people knowing they count in pursuing a clear and winning, even if challenging, strategy – the outcome of which they influence mightily. They flow from knowing that to the best of our ability we are living by our principles of winning with consumers and besting our competition as evidenced in clear cut performance superiority and building or certainly not losing share ... Every great leader inspires in his or her own way. It is not a matter of style. Taking the broader subject of passion, people have to know we, all of us, and especially their leaders, CARE about them as individuals.
>
> Needless to say "caring" without the right strategy and action plan will turn out to be hollow. In periods of great change, people need to know that change is in the name of a higher cause of helping the organization achieve its mission ... and there's no substitute for in-person contact.[4]

Or as Takeo Yamaguchi at Hitachi in Tokyo notes, "Even at headquarters, as I tried to set this new direction with a Japanese HR team that was in place before I arrived, I felt very alone. But then I brought in allies, from within and outside Hitachi ... I found new allies among our regional HR leaders in China, India, and the United States ... And together we've begun to convince the local leaders that we're doing the right thing."[5] Once the local leaders are on board with the new direction, that momentum will diffuse and empower and create excitement in others.

In this chapter, we drill down on how we can convert disengagement into passion, ownership, and action. Brilliant ideas for "what" changes to pursue are essential for Stragility, but the "how" of change is equally, if not more, important or those ideas will never succeed. Often, top executives are cast as "heroes" who will lead the organization to victory. Creating Stragility, by contrast, requires strategic leadership to be dispersed throughout the firm so that everyone in the organization has ownership and can be responsive and adept. A Stragility approach recognizes that while the content of change is critical for now, it will eventually become obsolete. The processes of change – the "how" – on the other hand, if managed well, will generate collective energy and passion that will help sustain the organization through subsequent changes. However, if the process is negative, not only will it make success unlikely for this change, but it can also tarnish changes yet to come.

Global Port Reinvention: From Rough Waters to Smooth Sailing

A great example of an organization that did a brilliant job of inspiring and engaging its people to take on a major strategic turnaround is one of the busiest international ports in the world, which we'll call Global Port. Global Port was starting to hit rough waters. After years of success, they were losing business to other ports and they were increasingly dependent on one cruise line. They needed to change what they did to attract new cargo and cruise ship business. As they looked at potential points of differentiation from other ports, Global Port realized that most of their competitors around the world had sufficient scale, easy access to transportation, attractive locations, and capacity for new business. Global Port needed to create a new source of competitive advantage. They decided to become the port that was easiest to cruise from and do business with. Under a "Smooth Sailing" positioning, they began looking at everything they did to see how they could make every aspect welcoming, hassle-free, and delightful.

They faced a skeptical workforce. Giovanni, who led the project, commented,

> Like employees everywhere, most people were afraid of the change. They'd been there a long time. They knew things needed to change to attract new business but they didn't know how. We knew that we needed to be with employees in face-to-face communication and not try to do this on email. To make the external transformation work, it had to be preceded by internal transformation – the workforce had to embrace the change. Employee engagement was the most important step in making the change happen. It removed the fear and got people excited about bringing the mission to life.[6]

The team developed a comprehensive employee engagement program. It included input meetings with a lead team of brand advocates from every part of the organization. They chose the "go-to" people who were key influencers, and they generated ownership by asking for their input on how the changes would affect their departments – both pluses and minuses. The team also tasked them to (1) share changes with their groups; (2) bring questions, suggestions, and concerns back to the core team; and (3) serve as ongoing ambassadors, relaying suggestions to further deliver on the port's Smooth Sailing mission.

The Smooth Sailing mission resonated with people. The meetings gave people a chance to share and develop their ideas and suggestions. Even the skeptics were pleased they had been consulted, and many started to buy in. The leadership team also uncovered points of resistance and areas where the plan needed to be fine-tuned. Many within Global Port were concerned about what this meant for their jobs. To make the new Smooth Sailing mission come alive and become a success, everyone would have to let go of old ways of working, begin collaborating across functions, and change how they all worked together.

Meanwhile, Human Resources rewrote job descriptions and measures to link them all to a hassle-free, pleasant experience. For example, logistics group work was redesigned to streamline the paperwork and include personalized follow-up and enhanced service levels for the biggest cargo and cruise lines. They studied where each process was getting bogged down and looked for ways to make it smoother. Unlike many change efforts that stop with high-level strategies, they worked end-to-end to redesign every operation of the port.

To launch the project, Global Port leaders held face-to-face town hall meetings with every employee in every department. They shared the new Smooth Sailing mission, purpose, and competitive positioning and discussed how and why it would help the port grow, thereby making employees' jobs more secure. They showed everyone the plans, which included a new logo, new uniforms, entertainment in the terminals, and more. Everyone was asked for their input and suggestions about how they could contribute to the new mission and purpose. Discussion then focused on how the changes would affect people's jobs. One parking lot attendant said he could act as a greeter, extending his parking duties to include helping people unload and starting their experience off right. Another suggested adding a play area to the waiting room, and a third suggested building stroller and wheelchair ramps to help everyone move around easily while waiting. As each person shared their thoughts, more came forward with new ideas.

"Once people understood the overall mission, they saw how they could do their job in a way that supported the mission. And they felt proud to be part of the transformation of their port," said Giovanni. The port secured several new cruise lines and cargo customers, has top ratings for hassle-free sailing, and now contributes over half a billion dollars annually to the local economy.

As the port learned, cultivating ownership, commitment, and creativity are essential for successful change and Stragility. People need to understand why the changes are necessary, have the skills and resources they need to contribute to the shift, and have leeway to make decisions and take actions that they believe will help move the organization in the right direction. If given that room to run, they can fully engage and leverage their talents to make the vision happen. By inspiring and engaging, we all can turn the rough waters of change to smooth sailing.

Ignite Passion through the "Why?"

Often people have insufficient understanding of *why* they need to change. We all know that it is hard for us to commit to something or take ownership if we don't know why we're supposed to do it. Yet in organizations where we spend much of our lives, we often expect people to dive in with head and heart without understanding the rationale behind the changes they're being asked to make.

A longtime executive in high-tech talks about the importance of what she calls aspiration and inspiration: "Every environment is different. What motivates changed behavior on a factory floor is different from what works in an R&D lab. What works in one company won't work exactly the same way in another. However, no matter what the environment, a vital starting point for motivating changed behavior is real agreement and real belief that improved performance is both necessary and possible."[7] She continues, "Nowhere are aspiration and inspiration more important than in a large, complex organization undergoing major change. In large companies, a myriad of actions taken and countless small decisions must add up to the bottom line. And in a period of change, each employee must break old habits and learn new skills, and every employee's actions and decisions must align in new ways to produce something different."[8]

Share the Vision and Business Case

At the core of every great strategic change are a compelling vision and business case, which create a persuasive rationale for why the company is headed in this new direction. Let's start with the vision. In many organizations, vision statements focus primarily on market and competitive positioning. The vision is more marketing promotion than inspirational. It often doesn't resonate internally. That makes it hard for those in the organization to know what to do.

But some organizations know how to combine aspiration and inspiration to make a winning combination that resonates for all stakeholders. Consider Whole Foods' mantra: "Whole Foods, Whole People, Whole Planet." Short, clear, simple. It emphasizes that their vision reaches way beyond just food retailing. As their website explains, their

> deepest purpose as an organization is helping support the health, well-being, and healing of people – customers, Team Members, and business organizations in general – and the planet. And our Core Values are not just words on a wall somewhere: they're guiding principles that inform every decision we make – from the daily, face-to-face interactions with our customers to larger decisions that impact the way Whole Foods Market evolves and grows. We encourage our Team Members to connect with our Core Values on a personal level, choosing the one(s) that are most meaningful to them and making them "come to life" in their work. It is empowerment in its truest sense, and we think it's what can make working at Whole Foods Market such a unique and rewarding experience.[9]

Now that feels inspirational and aspirational. We know what we're working toward and have a sense of purpose. We also have some freedom to do what we think is best. As with Whole Foods, a good vision statement gives us a personal and organizational compass that guides our decisions, choices, actions, and behaviors and keeps us moving toward our common goals. Energy and passion are the fuel that keeps our organizations fired up. Usually, that passion stems from more than the bottom line. For us to feel intense dedication, our work in organizations needs to matter. We all want the organizations we work for to contribute something meaningful, inspiring, and useful to the world.

One of the first things that helps to inspire and engage is to create a meaningful vision and accompany it with the business case, or the "why" of the strategic initiative, in a way that people at all levels can relate to and understand. You might be thinking, "I need to roll this change out now. I don't have the time to mess around with visions and the case for change." We've actually had executives tell us, "The troops don't need to know any more than their marching orders." We'd like to suggest that kind of command-focused leadership has some serious drawbacks. If the troops don't understand why they're moving, how what they're doing figures into the strategy, what they're headed toward, or what to do if things fall apart, the change is going to fail. It doesn't work for guerilla warfare. And it doesn't work in business, especially for those companies facing fast-paced contexts where speed and customer responsiveness can't be slowed down with slow, hierarchical decision-making.

Traditionally, companies that do share their case for change may also have handled this by focusing solely on strategic objectives, the business case, and financial impact. Other firms use the "burning platform" – that "we better change fast or we'll all die" idea – to motivate people to change. As John Kotter (Harvard change guru) and Dan Cohen (Deloitte Consulting principal) aptly note, while burning platforms may "produce movement," they also create panic, which shifts people toward focusing on self-preservation rather than organizational transformation.[10]

So what can we do? As the Global Port story illustrates, when we begin with a strong vision such as "smooth sailing," it is much easier for people to understand and engage. Global Port also did a great job of mapping and working with the political landscape (discussed in the last chapter). They consulted teams and departments in a cascading, two-way approach on what smooth sailing would mean for them and its benefits and drawbacks. Sponsors and promoters helped generate positive buzz about the changes they were launching. Positive and negative skeptics kept them alert for watch-outs (potential flaws or problem areas) and fine-tuned the "pitch" and action plan.

Connect with Story

Research shows that emotional connection – talking from the heart authentically and using stories – is much more likely to generate the enthusiasm and passion that moves people toward action and provide a sustaining purpose that keeps people working toward the vision.[11] Stories are much more memorable than facts. They help create deeper understanding and ignite a more powerful response. Good stories make us think and feel. Just think of the impact of the stories in this book. Our guess is that the stories we're telling here help make our ideas more concrete, memorable, and engaging.

Like the stories in this book, the stories we choose for the changes we lead should also transcend personal interest and short-run organizational benefits to focus on value creation – how taking action will create long-term value and help the organization and broader stakeholders win. Recent studies confirm that a focus on value creation rather than profit generates greater workforce engagement and superior financial results.[12]

We've learned a few principles about how to develop a compelling "why" story that ignites passion.[13] First, the story should resonate and demonstrate the reasons for heading in this direction. It should be grounded in a clear and compelling vision, as in the case of "Smooth Sailing." Fundamentally, what inspires most of us is joining together collectively to make a difference for ourselves, our organizations, and the world. Second, the story should emotionally connect with people. Rather than taking only a big-picture view, the story needs to show how the changes will impact those we serve. Third, it should include a call to action – what, specifically, each person should do to turn the vision into reality.

In addition to using stories to launch a change, gathering stories from around the organization can showcase and share leading practices and successes as the change rolls out. This helps ensure that people continue to connect emotionally with the change and see how the "why" of a change resonates with and is relevant to each individual. For example, Wynn Resorts in Las Vegas, Nevada, and Macau, China, knew its "delight the customer" approach was beginning to pay off when one of the waiters lent his own necktie to a patron who had forgotten his. They captured this story as part of their ongoing storytelling program to inspire their workforce at all levels to go the extra step. As they say, "Every employee has a great story of exceptional service to tell. Storytelling inspires each of us to find opportunities to create extraordinary experiences for our guests." Wynn Resorts gathers these inspiring stories in a number of different ways:

> The Story WIRE is a link on the WIRE, where you can submit your story electronically. Story CARDS are located in the back of house. You can pick one up, write

down your story and deposit it into the locked Storytellers Box. The Story PHONE is a special phone where you can record your name and details of your story. All stories are received, transcribed, and reviewed for future use. If your story is chosen, your photo and the story will be put together. Sometimes you'll see your story on a big display in the back of house. Sometimes you'll see it featured as a Story of the Week on the WIRE. Wherever it shows up, your story will inspire thousands of other employees.[14]

We also want to keep in mind the power of visualization. One large urban hospital in Australia was trying to reduce complexity and the number of suppliers they used to stock inventory. To illustrate the problem, they stacked a table in the staff lounge with hundreds of different brands of medical supplies being used, along with the question, "Do we really need 277 different suppliers?" People laughed and got the message.

Create a Mantra

A mantra expresses the essence of a brand in a few words. We are all likely familiar with mantras such as DeBeers' A Diamond Is Forever, LG's Life's Good, BMW's Ultimate Driving Machine, or Nike's Just Do It.

In the firms we worked with, we've found that change mantras can be powerful for anchoring strategic changes and initiatives as well. A change mantra should be an easy-to-share, memorable, inspiring guidepost of what the initiative or strategic shift is all about. They become a form of infectious messaging. These mantras help communicate the vision and purpose of the change, can generate buzz and awareness, provide a compass for the change, and help keep the change at the top of people's minds. Some companies even crowdsource their employees' ideas for what the mantra should be to help build engagement and ownership.

Did you notice how the vision of "Smooth Sailing" grabs our interest, tells us the end goal in a memorable way that sticks, and helps us envision changes in our own processes to create smoother sailing?

PricewaterhouseCoopers' plan to solve their female retention issue was called the "War for Talent" and linked to their mission-critical goal of attracting top performers. It also moved the company away from seeing the retention issue as a problem with "women." And P&G CEO A.G. Lafley used the mantra "Consumer Is Boss" to underscore that every decision, every action, should be evaluated with the consumer in mind.

The Japanese company Mitsubishi Electric uses "Changes for the Better" as a mantra that works both internally and externally. India's Infosys uses "Building Tomorrow's Enterprise." Even cities and countries are now using mantras. The city of Abu Dhabi, UAE, says, "And you think you've done it all?" and Egypt uses "where it all begins."

All these efforts can help put the organization in a more positive mindset. As Leslie Fieger, author, motivational speaker, and spiritualist, says, "Attitude is the difference between an ordeal and adventure."[15] How we frame things has much to do with how it transpires. A strong vision and business case combined with a story and mantra provide that uplifting frame on what we're doing and enables us to reach our goals and even beyond. On the flip side, when vision, business case, story, and mantra are missing, there's no rudder for the organization. There is no center, heart, and soul to the change.

Thus, story and emotional connection enable people to feel passion for the purpose rather than being more extrinsically motivated by rewards or fear and merely going through the motions. Particularly in hypercompetitive contexts, mantra and stories help anchor the change amidst the flux and chaos to drive determination, dedication, focus, and the belief that together we can accomplish our aspirations. Now that's a really powerful secret weapon that is unmatchable (see Stragility Tool 4-2).

Go Slow to Go Fast

Often we face quarterly reporting and other pressures, so we might be struggling with the idea of taking time for vision, developing a compelling business case, story creation, and a mantra. However, one of the most powerful learnings we see over and over again is that by going slower, we actually go faster. It seems counterintuitive, but taking the time to build passion, engage with people, help them understand, ask for ideas and input, work through their concerns, and map implications and details in the early days of a transition or turnaround increases the likelihood that the change will be successful and will actually be faster in the end.

That insight is echoed in a study by McKinsey & Company showing that the best way to build buy-in is to give the people most affected by change a role in shaping it.[16] High-performing companies know that change takes place through people. We need to ensure our people have input and ownership of what's happening, build their skills in the new behaviors, and have the flexibility to tailor the solution to their on-the-ground realities (see Stragility Tool 4-3). And we need to develop feedback loops, which we'll talk about more in the next chapter.

Let Go of the Past

In the classic French film *The Red Balloon*, a young boy discovers a stray balloon that seems to have a mind of its own. The two become inseparable, following each other all over Paris. The joy is short-lived. A gang of bullies destroys his balloon and the boy grieves its loss. But the loss precedes a magical new beginning as the sky fills up with red balloons lifting him toward new adventures.

Just like the little boy, we all learn that letting go of the past is part of moving forward. But that is often hard to do. For example, at one global company, a central group working on increasing the number of households served recommended discontinuing country-by country data gathering and analysis in favor of a global automated system based on the biggest countries and regions The local analysis was taking weeks of time, and by the time the data was analyzed, it was already outdated. Months later, they discovered that the data gathering and analysis was still happening locally. Why were the teams hanging on to their red balloons? Regional leaders had continued asking for the data by country, and the teams doing the analysis were being rewarded for it. They had not let go of the past system but continued to run it in parallel with the new global system.

In organizations, every change involves plenty of letting go. Organizations are constantly merging, acquiring or being acquired, downsizing, outsourcing, automating work processes, relocating teams, flattening organization structure, shifting technology, and integrating systems. Brenda Zimmerman, a complexity theorist and practitioner, noted that these shifts provide the creative destruction that fosters new growth.[17] However, through these changes, many of us experience fractured relationships, a decline in status or power, and a loss of a sense of competence or control of our destiny.

To understand these repercussions, we need to listen to those affected to understand their perspective, hopes, and fears. As the turn-of-the-century Nobel Prize—winning French author Anatole France said, "All changes, even the most longed for, have their melancholy; for what we leave behind us is a part of ourselves; we must die to one life before we can enter into another."[18]

As change leaders, we can help by giving people time to mourn, honoring the contributions of those who built the past, and letting them take a bit of the past with them. For example, we might give the team pictures or mementos of the old organization, let them take a brick from the factory that's closing, or create a ritual or event to mark the end of the old.

One top telecommunications executive learned about letting go from her moves every few years as a child to follow her professor dad to a new job. As she led her Network Systems team through a major change, she recalled those experiences.

> I remembered that every time I moved to a new city and a new school, I would be home-sick. The place I'd left seemed so much better. The people of the Network Systems were going to be homesick too. They were going to miss the way things used to be. I knew I'd have to work hard to keep their energies focused on where we were going because in their minds and in their conversations, they would keep returning to what they were leaving behind. And I knew from my own experience that it would be easier to face our future when everyone understood that we had no way to go "home" again.[19]

Provide the Resources, Skills, and Training Needed

Often overlooked roadblocks to change are lack of resources, skills, and training. If we want change to succeed, we must ensure that the people involved in the change have the necessary knowledge, understanding, and skills to become effective change leaders. They need to have the resources and training necessary to shape the change and build their sense of ownership whether through meetings, face-to-face training, mentoring, online resources, and video or printed materials. For example, many companies today have "embracing diversity" as one of their key values. But without resources, skills, training, and people's ideas on what that really means for leading, running meetings, hiring, and creative problem-solving, there will be a gap between the talk and the walk. And when people don't have what is needed, disengagement, blaming, inaction, and resentment often emerge as symptoms.

Christi Shaw, the US president of Switzerland-based Novartis Pharmaceuticals Corporation and winner of Diversity Inc's Top 50 Companies for Diversity several years in a row, including 2015, says, "Novartis Pharmaceuticals Corporation

is focused on creating products, services and solutions that help patients manage disease and live fuller lives. We believe that diversity and inclusion are
directly linked to the achievement of these goals – and can help us create a
culture where people can be authentic and courageous, where collaboration
can flourish, and where greater patient and customer understanding can drive
future breakthroughs and innovations."[20] Approximately 60 percent of Shaw's
direct reports are women. Novartis's strategy focuses on leveraging the diversity of patients, customers, and markets with diversity and inclusion embedded
in every aspect of Novartis, from new-product development, to clinical-trial
diversity, to commercialization and marketing, recruitment, onboarding, and
talent development. They have a vice president, head of Diversity & Inclusion;
19 employee resource groups; and an Executive Diversity and Inclusion Council
(EDIC), with the president and vice president of Diversity serving as co-chairs.
EDIC members represent each functional group and business organization
within the company. There also are Diversity and Inclusion Councils organized
by employees, who take responsibility for "infusing" diversity and inclusion
in their organizations and functions. In short, Novartis understands the business benefits of proactive diversity management and is devoting the necessary
resources to realize its diversity and inclusion goals.

Telling and selling without listening and providing adequate resources
doesn't work very well. Engaging and involving key stakeholders helps us figure
out what makes the most sense and how to provide specific skill-based training and resources to achieve the outcomes we are seeking. Another example
is TELUS, a large Canada-based telecommunications company. TELUS's strategic priority is to become the telecom industry's customer service leader.
They have revamped their internal systems and structures so that they can
bring their strategic priority – "listening to our customers and working hard to
ensure they are the happiest in the industry" – to life. Critical to their ability
to deliver exceptional customer value is their strategy of asking their stakeholders what changes would improve the customer experience rather than
telling them what they should do. For example, complex pricing strategies
are frustrating for both customers and customer relationship agents. An early
change TELUS launched to underscore their mantra of "Customers First" was
their launch of Clear and Simple Pricing, a straightforward set of all-in wireless
plans with no system access fee.

Internally, TELUS provides deep insights into the reality of the customer through their Closer to the Customer programs, where team members shadow those who work in front-line roles "to gain a more personal understanding of the experiences our customers have when interacting with TELUS. More than 12,000 team members have participated in this program since it was introduced in 2010."[21]

This customer and front-line input, along with incentives and metrics-reinforcing customer solutions, has led the company to introduce breakthrough customer-friendly changes, including rewriting its contracts in plain language; reducing international roaming rates by 60 to 80 percent; eliminating activation and renewal fees; introducing a simple smartphone trade-in program; having two-hour windows for arrival of technicians at people's homes for installation and service calls; and launching TELUS Neighbourhood, an online forum where customers can ask questions about their wireless or home services.[22]

As David Fuller, TELUS president of Consumer and Small Business Solutions, says, "Our team strives every day to put customers first, and our metrics confirm once again that TELUS is providing a truly differentiated experience and making the telecom industry a friendlier place for Canadians ... By embracing customer feedback and making real changes to meet their needs, TELUS has created customer loyalty that is amongst the highest for any telecommunications company around the globe. This is demonstrated by our industry leading postpaid wireless churn rate, which has been below one per cent for four consecutive quarters," and having the lowest complaint rate in the industry.[23]

As the Novartis and the TELUS stories illustrate, we need to ensure that everyone knows their strategic priorities and the overall game plan, has the needed resources, and then can provide input and take ownership for how their position will contribute to achieving the company's goals. Recall how the Global Port change leaders similarly worked with people to effectively launch "Smooth Sailing." Howard Schultz of Starbucks has said, "People want guidance, not rhetoric. They need to know what the plan of action is, and how it will be implemented. They want to be given responsibility to help solve the problem and authority to act on it."[24]

If things are derailing, we also need to understand where implementation is breaking down at the individual and work unit level. Do people not have the tools and skills to achieve change? Or perhaps they are so overloaded they don't have the time or capacity. Once we determine the outages, weak spots or opportunities, we can develop the right intervention plan.

One of most successful change programs of all time, Alcoholics Anonymous, doesn't ask members not to drink again, just not to drink that day. Weight Watchers follows a similar methodology, with awards for milestones like the first 5- and 10-pound weight loss. It is difficult to stay energized if there is no tangible evidence that our effort and time make a difference.

Unilever believes so strongly in employee engagement that they measure employees' brand engagement as a key performance indicator. They hold a series of "Big Moments" internal and external communication events to help engage employees and connect them with the company's purpose. Their goal is "inspiring people to take small, everyday actions that add up to a big difference."[25]

Communicate, Communicate, and Communicate

Most companies take their external communication strategy very seriously, thinking about the channels, format, and timing to reach customers most effectively. However, internal change communication typically includes email blasts, a video of the CEO, and a parade of meetings. To build passion and commitment, communication about change needs to be two-way and inspire people to do something new or different. We need to embed strategic intent in all elements of our internal marketing plans. There needs to be transparency about why we are changing and the benefit of short-term chaos. Using the stories and reasons for the change developed for "where are we going and why," tailored by and for different stakeholder groups, will also help bring the vision to life.

So in addition to having our external marketing plans developed, it's beneficial to think about the key marketing elements that must be in place *internally* to build awareness, engagement, and action among stakeholders. As David Novak, CEO of Yum! Brands, said, your turnaround strategy must be like a good ad, "memorable, engaging ... and makes you want to buy the product."[26] You must create ownership to keep employees invested in and excited about the success of the company.

While the specific nature of the communication is unique to each change, it's important that we are consistent and clear, have two-way communication opportunities, and use multiple channels to reach people in different ways. For example, one high-tech company had a multi-stakeholder task force to customize and communicate about change initiatives within different divisions. That was followed by a town hall meeting to launch the initiative with a powerful and inspirational CEO speech. Then they developed a video to create awareness. Parallel to these events, they created an intranet site and e-bulletin boards for basic information and FAQs, followed by a wiki to capture key concepts, frameworks, acronyms, and history.

As the change rolled out, they created "open speak sessions" to air performance gaps and create solutions, as well as weekly division and team meetings to solve problems, monitor progress, address issues, and solicit additional feedback. Throughout the change cycle, there was also an online newsletter to communicate upcoming events, results updates, and profile successes, along with blogs to share learning and feedback and user-generated ideas.

Thus, a robust communication strategy is critical. This dialogue is also helpful for learning how the change is unfolding from the ground up, sharing and diffusing leading practices and innovations that emerge, and showcasing successes that help fuel the process and sustain momentum (see Stragility Tool 4-3).

Stay Close to the Action

Often our view of change from a distance is far different from the realities on the ground. In Stevie Smith's famous poem, "Not Waving but Drowning,"[27] people on the shore wave to a swimmer far from shore who they think is waving back. Alas, she's "not waving but drowning." We need to be close enough to our organizations to see where they are struggling and hear their cries for help. As leaders, we should be out there in the field with our people, identifying ways to help remove barriers, reapplying things that are working, celebrating early wins, problem-solving together, and taking time to listen and actively solicit feedback. Unless we ask, they can't tell us.

Bill Marriott, founder of Marriott International, was famous for his listening skills and asking everyone what they thought, often learning the most from his housekeeping staff.

Distribute Ownership and Accountability

Good ideas bubble up and emerge continuously from people if we create the right conditions. Sometimes change can be sparked by ideas from the front line, sometimes by customers or other outside stakeholders, sometimes intentionally, sometimes unintentionally. Even if an organization attempts "big" strategic leaps led by top management, change usually plays out as ongoing, self-organizing, and emergent. Leadership is distributed across the organization as different people and their units are engaging in decisions and actions at different speeds. Leading strategic transformation and turnarounds is not about creating mechanisms for control. The best leaders create space for passion and ownership to flourish. They enable those who work with them to figure out what to do, how, and when in ways that they believe are best to achieve that vision. They foster and leverage the "collective wisdom" of the organization.[28]

As the retired president of P&G Europe, Wolfgang Berndt, said, "The key thing I am learning is the importance of not over controlling and over-regulating the business to leave room for entrepreneurial improvisation under the realities of the competitive marketplace." Or, as another top executive told us, "my goal is to always listen more than I talk."

Thus, another Stragility skill for inspiring and engaging our people around a strategic shift is learning how to share and decentralize ownership so that those actually carrying out the changes have the opportunity to shape and mold their actions. We find that letting people be responsible for how things are implemented builds skill sets and passion for both this change and subsequent changes. Shared leadership also enables speedier decision-making, needed for fast-paced business contexts. As we share ownership, each employee writes work plans that tie back into the overall mission, their roles, and their deliverables. For example, the bakery manager implementing a "freshness" strategy might include "restock shelves before each break" into his or her work plan.

So how might we do this? Let's take the all too familiar example of a company that needs to massively cut costs. That's one of the toughest change challenges out there and one most of us face frequently. Many of us are tempted in this situation to tell and sell. One company, Teranet, launched a major cost-cutting productivity initiative with a very decentralized, bottom-up approach. The question was how to inspire staff to be interested in cost savings, particularly since their long-tenured folks were naturally wary of any efficiencies that could theoretically lead to head-count reductions.

The solution was twofold. First, they made the initiative highly visible, with heavy incentives to perform. Cost savings was a corporate balanced scorecard measure, with a target of 150 implemented improvements. There were no restrictions on type or size of initiative – they wanted to encourage employees to focus on the little details and also make sure that everyone could contribute. Many managers were bonused partially based on this balanced scorecard measure. Additionally, this was one of the four measures determining the profit-sharing bonus that all employees are eligible to receive (essentially an additional two weeks' pay at the end of the year). Finally, they conducted periodic draws during town hall meetings, where they threw all the submitted initiatives into a hat and did a random selection to win a free coffee card or similar small item.

Second, they gave each department a rough quota and encouraged side bets and contests with other teams. Having these friendly rivalries and wagers helped encourage the teams to get into the action. They ended up with over 300 implemented improvements during this first year, doubling their target of 150. The company's head count is approximately 350, so they had nearly one improvement per employee on average. That's amazing engagement!

Last year, they kept a similar measure but changed the focus slightly to concentrate on improvements meeting a certain threshold, which was a cost savings of over $10,000 or cycle time improvement of over 25 percent. This was done for two reasons: to get staff thinking bigger and to encourage teamwork across departments. Most initiatives meeting that threshold would require the cooperation of multiple teams, so this worked well with another of their corporate priorities, which was to support enhanced teamwork. However, they kept the natural rivalries and side bets to maintain friendly competition. They again exceeded their target (20) with a total of 30 implemented improvements.[29]

This story is a beautiful example of decentralizing and sharing ownership for a strategic change and achieving incredible results from people even with a change as difficult as cost-cutting. We can also see how this approach fueled passion and engagement and how, by creating this success, the organization developed important Stragility skills for other upcoming challenges and changes (see Stragility Tool 4-3).

Provide Help and Hope

As change leaders, we need to be able to see the big picture from 20,000 feet above and also get down and dirty in the mud and provide help and hope. Sometimes, we need to help folks see how the changes we're embarking on connect to strategy, and sometimes we need to step into their shoes and see how things look on the ground (see Stragility Tool 4-3).

Legend has it that after a battle many years ago, a man in civilian clothes rode past a small group of exhausted, battle-weary soldiers digging an obviously important defensive position. The officer, making no effort to help, was shouting orders, threatening punishment if the work was not completed within the hour.

"Why are you are not helping?" asked the stranger on horseback.

"I am in charge. The men do as I tell them," said the officer, adding, "Help them yourself if you feel strongly about it."

To the officer's surprise, the stranger dismounted and helped the men until the job was finished.

Before leaving, the stranger congratulated the men for their work and approached the puzzled officer.

"You should notify top command next time your rank prevents you from supporting your men and I will provide a more permanent solution," said the stranger.

Up close, the officer now recognized General George Washington – as well as the lesson he'd just been taught.[30]

Starbucks: Re-inspiring One Barista at a Time

We'll close this chapter by sharing the story of CEO Howard Schultz's strategic turnaround of Starbucks. It is difficult to re-inspire and transform a failing organization that's filled with fear into one that's filled with hope and can recoup. But Starbucks did it. Starbucks's mission of "inspiring and nurturing the human spirit, one person, one cup and one neighborhood at a time," has been at the heart of their journey.

While Starbucks is again soaring, it wasn't in 2007 and 2008. Sales and profits were plummeting as customers left the brand for cheaper or better alternatives. The company's global operating income in April 2008 was down 26 percent, the largest decline in their history.

As Schultz explained to talk show host Oprah Winfrey, "We had lost our way," he said. "The pursuit of profit became our reason for being and that's not the reason that Starbucks is in business ... we're in the business of exceeding the expectations of our customers." Starbucks's decline was triggered by many factors, which Schultz called a "perfect storm of external pressures and self-induced imperfections."[31]

They had expanded too rapidly to 2,300 stores. They had poor internal accountability and outdated equipment, and they had made disappointing real estate choices. Most importantly, they had lost sight of their customer-centered mission. In an email to senior executives in 2007, Schultz slammed the "commoditization of the Starbucks experience ... We need to look into the mirror and realize it's time to get back to the core ... to evoke the heritage, the tradition, and the passion that we have for the true Starbucks experience."[32]

Although many leaders facing such a decline would be tempted to slash and burn, Schultz pondered how to maintain the brand and a culture of humanity as he closed stores, laid off employees, and then tried to reignite the company. What he did might seem crazy to many. He decided to create a galvanizing event to jumpstart the company change effort. He created a four-day retreat in the middle of a recession. He held it in New Orleans when the city was still recovering from Hurricane Katrina and invited 10,000 partners for a corporate pep rally and retreat. Why spend all that money to bring them all there? "For all the promise of digital media to bring people together, I still believe the most sincere, lasting powers of human connection come from looking directly into someone else's eyes with no screen in between."[33]

When they arrived at the airport, a marching band greeted them with signs that said "Believe." Each person was given welcome bags with five different unique schedules for five major events including informational sessions, round tables, and panels, as well as four huge interactive galleries designed to re-inspire people with the mission, values, operations, and new store management skills. There were community volunteer events to help hurricane-shattered New Orleans, four blocks of street fairs, and two big surprise announcements. T-shirts said "Onward" instead of Starbucks. "If done right, and it had to be done right, it would raise our company's level of personal accountability, passion and performance."[34]

The questions Schultz asked at the retreat are a powerful example of engaging employees to re-create a vision and then translate that vision into concrete changes every Starbucks employee could relate to:

- How can we create and improve the store experience which is our heritage and the foundation of the brand's identity?
- How might we expand on our value proposition that has always been about emotional and human connection?
- How should we strengthen our voice to better tell our story?
- How can the company extend its coffee authority beyond the stores?[35]

The criteria for selecting the best ideas were simple and profound:

- Will it make our people proud?
- Will this make the customer experience better?
- Will this enhance Starbucks in the minds and hearts of customers?[36]

As Schultz says, "I had to raise tens of thousands of spirits, engaging our partners in a shared purpose and then leading them toward a shared future. I recognized that many of our partners were burdened with fear. Fear of risk. Fear of public failure. And in an uncertain economy, fear of their own futures which were tied to the future of the company ... Starbucks was going to be courageous."[37]

Schultz offered reassurance that "things are going to get better." He asked for people to commit themselves personally to changes needed: "The power of this company is you." He and the management team then "got into the mud." They were accessible, almost ubiquitous – showing up, listening to and talking with Starbucks's partners and employees to identify inefficiencies and gather ideas for improvement – and they "threaded optimism into every communication."[38]

They grounded the changes in company vision, strategy, values, and culture and talked about what was *not* changing. "As we execute this transformation, there are certain integral aspects of our company that will not change at all. These include our commitment to treating each other with respect and dignity, providing health care and Bean Stock for all of our eligible full- and

part-time partners, and our commitment to our community efforts, our ethi-
cal sourcing practices and encouraging our coffee suppliers to participate in
our CAFE practices program in our origin countries."[39]

His goal? To "inspire" and to challenge employees to be personally accountable for everything at their stores. Ten thousand people left New Orleans with
"a tidal wave of energy." Since then, Starbucks shares have recouped. The
company has seen record revenue and profits and tripled their stock price. As
Schultz said recently, "When you're surrounded by people who share a pas-
sionate commitment around a common purpose, anything is possible."

Recap

Strategic turnarounds, shifts, and changes do initially feel chaotic. Too often,
when leaders fail to engage the organization, everyone emerges weaker,
resentful, stressed, and demotivated. But change done well, as the Global Port,
Teranet, and Starbucks stories illustrate, sparks energy, innovation, and passion
in the organization. These organizations emerge stronger and more resilient,
and they've developed essential skills of Stragility for succeeding now and into
the future. And as John Pepper so eloquently noted, people feel accountability
when they know they count and share ownership of a winning strategy.

Yes, strategic transformations and turnarounds involve lots of work and
always take longer than expected. They are also hard for people, emotionally
and in terms of workload, learning new skills and competencies, and regain-
ing confidence. Strategic change is a bit like seasonal change. We need to go
through winter (the chaos) to prepare for the rebirth and energy that spring
brings. And, like George Washington pitching in to dig a ditch, we need to roll
up our sleeves and help.

Recall how the interventions Schultz implemented at Starbucks inspired
and engaged. He kept stakeholders, including both employees and customers, at the front of his mind. Together, they ignited passion with a customer-
focused vision. They connected with stories and created a mantra – "Believe."
Schultz also went slow to go fast. He trusted his people and took the time and
expense to have this week-long retreat in New Orleans. He gave people an
opportunity to provide input, he distributed ownership to his people, and he
learned from them how to reinvent the company as he iterated the high-level
plans and the ground-level realities.

STRAGILITY DIAGNOSTIC TOOL 4-1:
Fostering Ownership and Accountability: From Tell and Sell to Inspire and Engage

Stragility Diagnostic	Green / Yellow / Red	Getting Started
Check the appropriate box: green = good, yellow = needs work, red = major opportunity		
Do people understand our compelling vision, business case, and benefits of this strategic change?	☐ ☐ ☐	**Stragility Tool 4-2 Igniting Passion**
Are we using mantras, stories, and powerful visualizations to engage and inspire our key stakeholders in these changes?	☐ ☐ ☐	**Stragility Tool 4-2 Igniting Passion**
Are we building In rituals to help our people let go of the past?	☐ ☐ ☐	**Stragility Tool 4-3 Fostering Ownership and Accountability**
Are we facilitating our team's ability to drill down on the specifics, creating ownership, flexibility, and accountability?	☐ ☐ ☐	**Stragllity Tool 4-3 Fostering Ownership and Accountability**
Have we brainstormed, prioritized, and filtered our ideas to come up with the best this-day-forward actions	☐ ☐ ☐	**Stragility Tool 4-3 Fostering Ownership and Accountability**
Have we designed a communication strategy that is two-way, multi-channel, and engaging?	☐ ☐ ☐	**Stragility Tool 4-3 Fostering Ownership and Accountability**
Have we asked our stakeholders how to build the change into their work plans, measures, and incentives?	☐ ☐ ☐	**Stragility Tool 4-3 Fostering Ownership and Accountability**
What are we doing to provide help and hope?	☐ ☐ ☐	**Stragility Tool 4-3 Fostering Ownership and Accountability**

STRAGILITY TOOL 4-2:
Igniting Passion with the Compelling "Why?"

With input from key influencers, build the business case and benefits based on external and/ or internal diagnostics to create a compelling "why" for the change and tie to value creation.

Develop story (tie into stakeholder stories), mantra (three-word capture), and powerful visualizations that will connect, resonate, energize, and create "buzz."

Share the vision and this compelling and infectious "why," communicating with authenticity.

Key Influencers to Enroll   **Business Case**   **Benefits**

Stories to Leverage   **Mantra**   **Powerful Visualizations**

STRAGILITY TOOL 4-3:
Fostering Ownership and Accountability

Let Go of the Past	How can we help people feel good about past accomplishments?	What ceremonies, rituals, celebrations will help transitioning to the future?

Develop Omnichannel Communications Strategy	Channel	Purpose	When?
Which channels or forms of engagement will be used for which stakeholders or activities and when?	e.g., online newsletter	e.g., track progress, post FAQs	

Distribute Ownership and Responsibility for Drill Downs	Define scope and use project management templates. Build into work plans and performance measurement.
Who? Change champions and teams	
What?	
How?	
Where?	
When?	

Offer Help and Hope	What resources, skills, and training are needed?	Other sources of support that should be provided?

chapter five

Creating Successful Change Again and Again: From Change Fatigue to Change Fitness

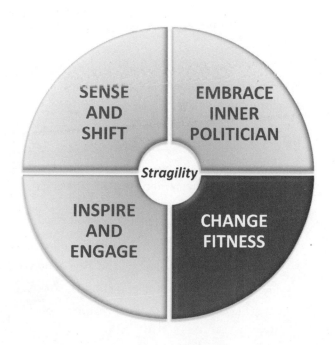

Stragility Skill

Change Fitness

Stragility Success Principles

Change Less and Achieve More

- Sunset teams, task forces, and projects
- Prioritize and bundle

Run Water through the Pipes

- Pilot and prototype
- Conduct pre-mortems and contingency plan

Pace and Get the Rhythm Right

- Punctuate with quick wins and milestones
- Choose smart timing

Be the Change

- Manage energy, not time
- Remove energy drainers and avoid head bangers
- Bounce forward from setbacks

Learn to Learn

- Dedicate time for introspection and after-action reviews
- Capture and track stakeholder feedback
- Connect diverse people to foster reapplication

Burnout doesn't happen because we're solving problems, it occurs be-
cause we're trying to solve the same problem over and over.

Susan Scott[1]

Satisfaction comes from stability
Happiness comes from acceptance
Greatness comes from change

Lindsey and Shannon Auster-Weiss

The book *Winnie-the-Pooh* begins, "Here is Edward Bear [also known as Win-nie-the-Pooh], coming downstairs now, bump, bump, bump, on the back of his head, behind Christopher Robin. It is, as far as he knows, the only way of coming downstairs, but sometimes he feels that there really is another way, if only he could stop bumping for a moment and think about it."[2]

Don't we all sometimes wonder how much better things could be if we could just stop bump, bump, bumping along long enough to think about what we're doing and find a better way? Most of our organizations are a frenzy of activity, leaving us too frequently feeling Pooh Bear's frustration. We're focusing on the tactical level, firefighting and reacting while juggling deadlines with a whirlwind of meetings, emails, texts, and conference calls. It's easy for us to fall into the bad habit of just trying to get it done and survive. But that typically leads to a downward spiral. We all too often become exhausted and burned out.

But change never stops, and the pace often overwhelms people's ability to cope. Not only will this change we are leading need to morph as it rolls out, but another change will not be far behind. Most of us have many changes on our plates, both work and personal, that we are trying to manage. So how can we handle it all and avoid personal and organizational burnout? To achieve sustainable success we must not only navigate through every current initiative and change; we must also build the ongoing capabilities required for continuous learning and evolution. That's what we call change fitness.

This chapter focuses on the final step in Stragility and how we can help ourselves and our organizations avoid change fatigue and create change fitness. It may be the most critical of the Stragility skills, without which we're all just bouncing down stairs on our heads. To create change fitness, we need change less so we can accomplish more. We can do this by sunsetting, or shutting down projects that are no longer important, and by prioritizing the critical projects that remain. We can also run water through the pipes by testing and piloting on a smaller scale before rolling out and developing contingency plans.

Like a good athlete, we also must pace ourselves and get the rhythm right. Having a sense of calm strength throughout is key. With relentless change, everything we do offers us opportunities to practice and continually improve the Stragility skill of change fitness.

Dematic Delivers for Its Customers: Putting Stragility into Practice

Few companies have withstood the amount of change that Dematic has.[3] Yet Dematic is not only surviving, it is thriving. See if you can spot the principles they applied to achieve their ongoing success. The venerable 75-year-old conveyor belt firm has been hit by technological transformation, revolutions in supply-chain management, and global low-cost competitors from China and the Philippines. Their external world has also been transformed by what they call the "Amazon effect." People want their goods shipped for free and available in 24 hours. And on top of all of this, they've changed ownership half a dozen times since the family of the founder sold it in 1980. It's been owned by big German firms Mannesmann AG and Siemens and by various private equity firms. With these new owners, even their name changed multiple times.

When current North American president and CEO John Baysore was hired in 2007, sales were down by more than two-thirds and nearly half the staff had been laid off. Things went from bad to worse, according to Baysore: "When I came on board, our competitors had just raided our camp and hired a bunch of people." The remaining staff was exhausted and demoralized as layoffs continued.

Baysore quickly realized he had to rally his people around a new customer-focused vision for the company and shift away from their current primarily internal manufacturing-oriented approach. Baysore had to bring back pride in the company and make it a magnet for top talent engineers, IT people, and project managers. This old manufacturing company needed to change rapidly to an engineering and project management company. To do this, he identified key influencers and rallied everyone around a new customer-centric vision: "All of our successful customers are successful in part because of what we do for them. We make them leaner, faster, more agile, able to handle more peaks and valleys, more accurate for their customers."

They reorganized and hired or retrained people with new skill sets to deliver the desired "Amazon effect." Dematic now develops software, storage, conveyor, sorting, and palleting systems for warehouses and distribution centers. These automated systems help their customers get their goods from production sites to storage sites and to the end consumer. And 75 percent of the company's workforce is now professional – mostly engineers, often the top talent from local universities. Dematic reframed customer needs to go way beyond automating supply lines, offering integrated supply-chain solutions to deliver products quickly and efficiently while saving on labor and space.

They brought back the pride in the organization and re-engaged some skeptics by naming one of its big new products Rapistan – the old company name. One of its many owners had forbidden employees to mention the old company name. When Baysore announced the return to Rapistan, tears welled up in his eyes as employees rose from their seats in a spontaneous standing ovation. People were delighted that, despite all the changes, they still had connections to their heritage.

They also brought back their "Little Red Schoolhouse" training center from the 1960s for use in their marketing materials. To further support employees, they added a fitness center and remodeled the cafeteria to add a café with computers and TVs. This made it easier for employees to gather and get to know each other. These employees have risen to the challenge of change after change and succeeded. Based on their improvements, they have recently won industry "Innovation" and "Top Service Provider" awards.

The company continues to change and grow, recently acquiring two new firms and branching out into new offerings like after-market services. Their customers include Amazon, Walmart, Frito-Lay, and Meier grocery stores. In North America, they now employ almost 3,000 people and generate about $900 million in revenues. And they command an astounding 40 percent share of the conveyance and sorting market.

If we wander into the Dematic Company, chances are we'll see signs of a fit company. People are gathered in the café discussing the latest acquisition, or in conference rooms energetically trying to figure out how to cut shipping costs even further for their customers, or laughing at lunch over how many twists and turns it took to solve a particularly thorny challenge. Dematic employees are just as busy as those in other companies, but they seem more rested; they filter their "to-do" lists through the lens of their mission to serve customers better. And they take time to recharge, to prioritize, to learn, and to celebrate success along the way.

Did you spot how they applied the lessons of the previous chapters? They redefined winning with a new vision and strategy. They watched their wings and sensed and shifted to discover the "Amazon effect," which required a new business model. They worked with people's fears and mobilized key influencers to bring everyone on board. They inspired and engaged employees while building support to make the change happen, and they are building-change fitness into their approach to ensure they are able to keep their performance optimized.

So how can we help our organizations achieve change fitness?

Change Less and Achieve More

Some companies change too much, others change too little or change the wrong things. It's important to understand what has made our firm successful in the past and incorporate successful business model elements in our changes going forward.

One of the more surprising findings in *Great by Choice*, Jim Collins's book based on research on "10xer" companies (firms providing shareholder returns at least 10 times greater than their industry over 15 years), is that these companies outperformed competitors by changing *less* than the comparison companies. Companies like Amgen, Biomet, Intel, Microsoft, Progressive Insurance, Southwest Airlines, and Strykerto – in contrast to less successful, "control" companies in the same industries, such as Genentech, Kirschner, AMD, Safeco, PSA, and United States Surgical – were unbeatable year after year by staying true to their business model.

For example, in Southwest's case, these core capabilities are flights under two hours, low fares, family service, fun, fast turnaround, simple processes, and decentralized ownership and accountability. If you've ever flown Southwest, you'll know what we're talking about. Air travel is so much more pleasant when your empowered flight attendant jazzes up the usually dull pre-flight safety speech to make it both fun and effective. Take, for example, a recent flight from San Francisco to Chicago, with a flight attendant who kicked off his boarding instructions with this: "In the event you haven't been in an automobile since 1960, flight attendants still have to show you how to fasten a seatbelt."[4]

Just like these "10xers," to create change fitness, we need to understand the business models that have made us successful and simultaneously be in tune with changing customer needs and external trends that require fundamental business model shifts like those at Dematic.

Sunset Teams, Task Forces, or Programs to Free Up Capacity

In most organizations, we're so busy building and adding things that we often forget to ask what we should stop doing. Pretty soon our project lists are full of good projects no one has enough time to make great. As Joan Lewis, former P&G Global Officer and SVP of Consumer and Market Knowledge, said, "Hundreds or thousands of projects are good ideas but if we don't prune the list, they will strangle each other like weeds in a garden."[5] This is a major cause of burnout and change fatigue. Nothing is taken off our plates while the pile of things to do gets bigger and bigger. When was the last time any of us had a meeting where the purpose was to identify what to stop or unload or undo? Interestingly, one company we've worked with holds regular "work out" sessions to identify what work can be stopped.

When Steve Jobs returned as Apple CEO in 1997, the company was three months from being insolvent. Jobs reviewed hundreds of projects and shut 70 percent of them down. As Walter Isaacson tells the story in his book about Steve Jobs, "Finally, after a few weeks of reviews, he'd had enough. 'Stop!' he shouted at one big product session. 'This is crazy.' He grabbed a magic marker, padded to a whiteboard, and drew a horizontal and a vertical line to make a four-squared chart. 'Here's what we need,' he continued. Atop the two columns he wrote 'Consumer' and 'Pro'; he labeled the two rows 'Desktop' and 'Portable.' Apple's job, he said, was to make four great products, one for each quadrant." He forced the company to focus. After several years of losses, the company became profitable again.[6]

Walk into any grocery store and you'll see a great example of too many offerings adding up to a miserable shopping experience as manufacturers keep adding new items. To counter this trend, Costco CEO W. Craig Jelinek has spearheaded a regular "weed and feed" of their Kirkland private label products, holding each to high standards and discontinuing those that don't make the cut. "It must be as good or better in quality than the comparable branded item, and it can be offered to our members at a price at least 20 percent lower than we would sell the branded item. We try to ensure all of our members are able to try the new item through our demo/sampling program. After nine months to a year, we measure its weekly sales generated per building. If it doesn't meet targets, we delete the item."[7]

At Apple and Costco, sunsetting work to focus has been key. As we look at our own corporate priorities, do we know the three or four most critical projects? What work can we sunset?

Prioritize and Bundle

Another way we can reduce overload and change exhaustion is to prioritize and bundle together new initiatives we're launching.

Try our Prioritization Matrix followed by our Impact Matrix to help your team prioritize and weed. Draw a 2-by-2 matrix with the probability of success on one axis and probability of impact on the other axis, as show in Step 1. That's the first Prioritization Matrix. Then have those involved (hopefully a multi-stakeholder team) write key initiatives down on Post-it Notes and place them

Step 1: Prioritization Matrix

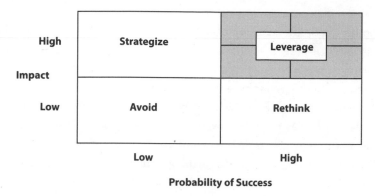

Step 2: Assessing Risk and Cost of Priorities in the Leverage Quadrant

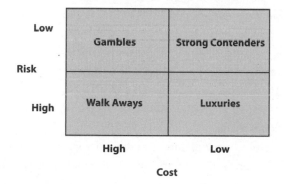

in the appropriate quadrant. This is a collective strategy for sorting what will yield the high-impact/high probability of success priorities or what our high-leverage priorities should be (upper right-hand corner).

We can then take the priorities in the "leverage" quadrant and further drill down by positioning in the matrix the highest impact and highest success targets using risk and cost, as shown in Step 2. This process will hone our strategic focus and generate our gambles and walk-aways that we might let go of, strong contenders to pursue, and luxuries that are costly but may be worth it. Both of these prioritization matrices will help prevent throwing good money after bad with sunk-cost initiatives and clear the decks of unfeasible options.

Another tactic for reducing change fatigue is to look for where we can bundle initiatives together. Often organizations have many related initiatives happening simultaneously that could be streamlined to help reduce change overload and burnout. Bundling is about finding connections with current initiatives already in the works. By bundling, we can sometimes simplify efforts and create a bigger bang. For example Sony PlayStation typically bundles upgrades with new games and new features.[8] And smartphone manufacturers like Samsung have done the same thing by bundling many innovations into each generation of their Galaxy Smartphones. We can apply the same idea of bundling internally when leading change. For example, we might have an overarching umbrella theme connecting all the changes in a particular year. One large global company we worked with had a theme one year of finding new ways to encourage innovation, called "Lightbulbs." Throughout the organization, people were encouraged and incentivized to find activities, policies, and practices that helped fuel new ideas, whether it was reapplying ideas across regions or restructuring practices to facilitate cross-functional pollination. This not only fostered creativity, it also provided a way to bundle a number of activities that were happening already but not connected. These initiatives were added in and thus built on the theme rather than added on, creating additional stress.

Thus, it's helpful to think about changing less to achieve more. By building on our strengths, sun setting, prioritizing, and bundling so we add in instead of add on, we can be more streamlined and focused, which helps alleviate change fatigue and makes strategic transitions feel less overwhelming.

Run Water through the Pipes

We can save ourselves time, energy, and resources by running water through the pipes to test and work out the kinks and by piloting our ideas experimentally in one area, department, or division before scaling up. Becoming comfortable with learning from pre-mortems and contingency plans also enables us to proactively anticipate consequences and fine-tune (see Stragility Tool 5-2).

Experiment and Conduct Rapid Prototyping

Conducting pilots and experiments helps to reduce risk and adjust before launching change more broadly. This trial-and-error process allows us to "run water through the pipes" to ensure the process works and that there are no blockages in the system. For example, a leading global bank undergoing major technological transition of their online banking system ran water through the pipes with parallel systems for several months, providing UATs (user acceptance training to work out bugs) and training all employees on the new system before making the transition. When they did transition, they reran Friday's work on a long weekend so they had time to fire-fight and adjust before Tuesday morning. They succeeded where a competitor had failed doing the same type of changeover. The botched change experienced by the competitor created a computer glitch that meant customers didn't have access to their accounts for over three days. It took months for the competitor bank to restore customer confidence after the reputational damage. Meanwhile, our best-practice bank that had run parallel systems got through the transition without a hitch.

Conduct Pre-mortems and Contingency Plan

We also want to consider what to do if something goes wrong and ensure we have backup or contingency plans to address these events. Pre-mortems are valuable before launches to force us to think through what might happen and better prepare ourselves to respond.[9] Pre-mortems might involve asking a multi-stakeholder group (including sponsors, promoters, and fence-sitters as well as positive and negative skeptics) to pretend "it's six months from now and the project has succeeded; why did it work so well?" Then also ask, "Now pretend it's six months from now and the project has failed; why did it nosedive?"

For example, one company was looking into launching a home dry-cleaning product. They did a pre-mortem and imagined that if dry cleaners attacked the product, it would not be successful. Based on this they positioned the product as a supplement to dry cleaning, not a replacement for it. As part of this planning we should anticipate dips in performance while people learn new skills and factor this into our estimates. The unexpected happens. Things fall apart. Upturns usually take longer than we think. That's where checking our lead metrics such as error rates or orders versus a year ago can be beneficial.

Interestingly, NASA (National Aeronautics and Space Administration) in the United States, continuously trains their astronauts with extreme pre-mortems in the form of space simulations. Chris Hadfield, a highly decorated astronaut who has flown about 2,336 orbits around earth and 62 million miles, and spent five months on the International Space station, explains that a heavy component of space training is preparing for the worst so you don't panic.[10] Every astronaut, as part of training, does hundreds of simulations, which include planned curveballs and also totally unexpected "green cards" – randomly triggered extreme crises that often occur back to back and escalate. These pre-mortems in the form of catastrophic scenarios enable astronauts like Chris Hatfield to know they have the problem-solving skills they need to handle whatever might arise.

Chris calls this the "power of negative thinking." "Death sims" (simulations), as he calls them, are "weirdly uplifting." Careful thinking and introspection about the realities of these possible scenarios in the form of pre-mortems and training are essential for a safe and successful space journey. The same is true for organizations; anticipatory introspection often can reveal valuable information that can be preemptively managed or may prompt us to make better, different choices.

Pace and Get the Rhythm Right

Prioritizing and finding the right pacing and rhythm are other Stragility skills that are critical for change fitness. Regardless of the specifics of change, most changes should be punctuated with quick-win phases and have the right timing, pacing, and sequencing. Instead of doing everything at once and maxing out (getting injured like an athlete who goes all out), we need to chunk it up into crawl, walk, and run phases. For example, during the HP merger with Compaq, they split the integration work into three phases. Phase I was about aspiration and unification of "a thousand tribes" into one organization with common market leadership aspirations. Phase II was about consolidation and integration, picking the best from each company. And Phase III was about lever-aging resources to win in the market.[11] By pacing, the organization was able to learn from failures and adjust, then celebrate progress on their journey.

Punctuate with Quick Wins and Milestones

Most of us need short-term goals and milestones to sustain our interest and keep our momentum. Therefore, as change leaders, we need to punctuate our work with quick wins that can be celebrated. Milestones, often called "dates with destiny" can focus, energize, and create urgency for the change.

Mapping out initiatives in an Impact/Time Matrix can be a useful tool for identifying and sorting out possible quick-win candidates. This time, create one axis called "impact" and the other called "time," as shown in Step 3. Note that this matrix can be used whenever the journey needs a jumpstart, not just at the beginning.

We can then filter our ideas by impact and time to identify back burners, quick wins, low-hanging fruit, and home runs (see Step 3). Back burners are those options we may want to percolate further because it's not clear whether they will have a high impact. Low-hanging fruit is quick and easy stuff we can do to move things forward. Quick wins are high impact and can be achieved sooner rather than later. Home runs are high-impact initiatives that might take several base hits and some time to launch.

Step 3: Timing and Pacing – Quick Wins

	Sooner	Later
High Impact	Quick Wins	Home Runs
Low	Low Hanging Fruit	Back Burners

Time

Smart Timing

We've identified high priorities, bundled, conducted pilots and pre-mortems, and built in pacing and quick wins as well as milestones. We think we're doing everything right, and then it all blows up because we launched in the busiest season of the year. For example, one major retailer in Brazil tried to do a major store redesign right in the middle of the Christmas season. Check the timing with suppliers and customers too, who also are likely simultaneously managing multiple change initiatives. What else is on their plates could affect how successful our initiatives will be.

Be the Change

The lesson to put our own oxygen mask on first before assisting others is one that can be applied beyond airplanes. Change always begins one person at a time; as change leaders, it must begin with us. People need to see our positive energy and our real belief that change is both necessary and possible. Part of our job as leaders is to help our people have a mindset that fuels success and helps those we work with to tap into their strength and their confidence in their ability to tackle change again and again.

It is a demanding job. We all need to find ways to recharge ourselves, weather the inevitable crises and failures, and bring consistent high, positive energy to work. One of the things both of us (the authors) have learned, through meditation and yoga, is the power of our minds in framing how we react to things. In other words, the same stuff framed and faced differently can lead to dramatically different outcomes.

For most of us, dedicating endless hours to meditation and stress relief isn't a viable option. The great news is that some simple techniques can enable us to cultivate inner calm and personal health and positivity. These include focusing on managing our energy, not our time, directing our energy to where we can actually have an impact, removing energy drainers and head bangers, and discovering how to bounce forward from setbacks.

The best leaders know that people will take their cues from us. Cultivating and projecting inner calm can have a huge impact. Think about how Nelson Mandela was unflaggingly optimistic that South Africa could and would become a place for all races and all people to thrive. While others were pre-dicting a meltdown, Mandela's confidence was critical for inspiring confidence in others. He also took steps to energize himself and celebrate along the way:

> I have walked that long road to freedom. I have tried not to falter; I have made missteps along the way. But I have discovered the secret that after climbing a great hill, one only finds that there are many more hills to climb. I have taken a moment here to rest, to steal a view of the glorious vista that surrounds me, to look back on the distance I have come. But I can rest only for a moment, for with freedom comes responsibilities, and I dare not linger, for my long walk is not yet ended [12]

One company that is trying to help executives put on their own oxygen masks and learn the skills of change fitness is MasterCard. Nearly every aspect of their business model has changed in the last few years. Before its IPO in 2006, MasterCard was a nonprofit owned by 25,000 banks. They are now a public company confronting changes in an increasingly non-cash-centric world, where digital and mobile are replacing plastic and consum-ers expect more and more services from their credit card. Their CEO, Ajay Banga, has focused on transforming internally to help his organization achieve greater market focus externally. He has developed an executive leadership program to build the change fitness of his leaders. Centered on helping leaders understand "the primary responsibility in the transforma-tion of the business and that the urgency to make it happens lies with them," the program is taught by senior leaders and includes assessments, coaching, teaching, and dialogue.[13]

Manage Energy, Not Time

A lot of recent studies are finding convincing evidence that energy, not time, is the fundamental currency of high performance, not only for world-class athletes but also for business professionals. Though no surprise to any of us who have been in business for decades, but perhaps a surprise to others, the performance expectations of business leaders are *much* greater than for ath-letes. Athletes have off-seasons and are expected to be top performers for 5–10 years and then move on. They cultivate routines that involve oscillating between activity and rest, training and recovery.

As business leaders, we are increasingly expected to perform at our peak for 30 or 40 years. We're expected to be available 24/7, always "on" through endless meetings and projects. To cope, we multitask, eat poorly, and cut back on family, physical, and spiritual activities to focus on the mental and emotional demands of our work lives. And we don't build in time for recovery. Doing this too long, we "flatline" – with low energy and motivation. This tends to set the tone for the rest of the organization.

Jim Loehr and Tony Schwartz, who founded the Energy Project, work with companies such as Google, Coca-Cola, Green Mountain Coffee, the Los Angeles Police Department, Cleveland Clinic, and Genentech on leveraging personal energy and renewal. Interestingly, in their initial work with top-ranked tennis players like Monica Seles and Pete Sampras, Jim and Tony found no difference in how well top performers played a particular point versus those tennis players who were struggling. It is only when they looked at what these people were doing *between* points and outside the matches that the differences became clear. The top performers took advantage of the short time between points to recharge. And they built routines of intense training punctuated with periods of rest and recovery. They relied on four sources of energy: physical with good diet and fitness, emotional with stress reduction techniques, mental focus during performance, and spiritual grounding with life mission, values, and purpose.

Both groups had the same amount of time in the day, but the top performers leveraged their energy to get much more success out of the time they had, with less time lost to anger and moodiness or dysfunctional thinking. They thought of their life as a series of sprints rather than an always-on marathon. The most successful high performers learned how to spend and renew energy throughout their days and their lives. Roger Federer is a great example of a high performer who manages energy well.

We all can improve how we manage our personal and organizational energy to balance expenditure and renewal. Consider taking a little nap or getting a good night's sleep a waste of time? A recent Stanford study found that when male basketball players slept 10 hours a night, their performances in free-throw and three-point shooting each increased by an average of 9 percent. Similarly, when night-shift air traffic controllers took an average nap of just 19 minutes, they performed much better on tests that measured their ability to monitor flights and reaction time. Longer naps have an even more profound impact than shorter ones. A sleep researcher at the University of California, Riverside, found that a nap of an hour or an hour and a half increased memory recall equal to sleeping eight hours.[14] Sleep can restore our memory. We've talked throughout this book about the importance of focus, adaptability, creativity, smart decision-making, and keeping things in perspective. Interestingly, most of those functions are located in the cerebral cortex, part of the frontal lobe of our brains, which is the first to falter if we're behind on sleep. The sleep-deprived are more likely to make errors, be rigid, be less creative, be distracted, and lack good judgment, all traits that are pretty counterproductive for Stragility.[15]

As the founding dean of the Schulich Business School Jim Gillies astutely noted, "we can get more done in 11 months, than we can 12." In other words, by taking a month off, we'll be more energized and accomplish more than if we worked 12 months straight. The evidence certainly supports that view. Ernst & Young found that each additional day of vacation taken by their employees yielded an 8 percent increase in their end-of-year performance ratings and that those who took their vacations were also significantly less likely to leave the firm. Americans on average leave more than a week of vacation days unused each year. So while most people don't take the full vacation time they're allocated, we should.[16]

As leaders, we are often stewards of organizational energy, mobilizing, investing, channeling, and expanding the energy of our teams. Many companies have institutionalized practices like transcendental meditation or fitness centers to help employees build recovery into their days. And they are encouraging employees to take their vacations. What some people would call "slacking off" successful organizations such as Google and Facebook realize are energy-generating activities that yield huge performance returns. A recent McKinsey survey of executives showed that 42 percent of companies that aspired to transform their health along with their performance were very or extremely successful in meeting their goals, compared with only 27 percent of those that aimed to change performance alone. In addition, companies that included health-focused initiatives were twice as successful as the others.[17]

Need a good idea? Don't wait at your desk for the proverbial light bulb to light up. Simply going for a walk increases creativity by over 60 percent versus sitting at a desk.[18] In fact, most people say that great ideas come to them when they are doing something else. Walt Disney sketched his first Mickey Mouse on a trip from New York to Hollywood, and J.K. Rowling dreamed up Harry Potter while stuck on a stalled train.[19] So the next time we feel stuck, having a "walking meeting" might yield an exciting and innovative solution.

Indeed, as we wrote this book, we didn't lock ourselves in a room and bang out the pages. We consciously worked hard, sometimes on laptops but other times playing with ideas with Post-its on flip charts. We also deliberately took "breaks" such as walking, swimming, yoga, and bicycling. While that might look like unproductive time, those rechargers were the energizers that enabled us to brainstorm and generate breakthrough ideas. We also simply moved away from the table we were working at to other spaces or locations or moved to flip charts to change things up. Varying how and where we worked helped us manage our energy and made our thinking and writing more creative and more efficient.

As an example, one company has centered their culture and energy renewal around a kitchen table. The ad agency Droga5, which was just awarded Advertising Age's A-List award, says their creative culture is key to their stellar results. That culture starts in their kitchen, where new staffers are welcomed and where teams gather to discuss challenges. They build in fun and work toward a "funkiness" and "scrappiness" culture. There's dinner every night, with "Pizza Thursday" celebrations each week. "The kitchen table approach is emblematic of how Droga5 works, even as it expands." And business results have followed. The company has had seven straight years of 30 percent growth.[20]

Remove Energy Drainers and Avoid Head Bangers

Creating inner calm also means trying to avoid or remove energy drainers. Energy drainers can be management layers, career competition, and inconsistent technological platforms or anything that frustrates us but is out of our control.

The Serenity Prayer by Reinhold Niebuhr (a theologian and philosopher) holds so much wisdom on change: "grant me the serenity to accept the things I cannot change, courage to change the things I can, and wisdom to know the difference." This prayer encourages us to focus on those activities within our circle of control and influence.

"Head bangers" is a term we like to use for those issues that we keep fighting even when we realize they are unlikely to shift at the current time.

Maybe we don't agree with a decision that has been made by higher-ups. We gave our input but the organization went with another's point of view. Rather than keep raising the issue, it's better now to see what we can do to make it successful. One organization has a mantra related to this: "Agree, disagree, commit." This encourages healthy debate but also sets the expectation that once a decision is made, those in the organization will commit to making it happen.

In short, it is far more effective to focus on areas where we can have an impact and let go of those that are out of our control or outside our circle of influence. The Dalai Lama XIV captures this well: "If a problem is fixable, if a situation is such that you can do something about it, then there is no need to worry. If it's not fixable, then there is no help in worrying. There is no benefit in worrying whatsoever."[21]

It is also helpful to remember that we can always choose how we react even if we can't control or shape what's happening. In a crisis, angry eruptions probably won't be beneficial for those around us. A better approach would be to take a walk, take a little time, pause, and breathe. We should also help those who work with us to develop the same sense of inner calm.

We build change fitness by taking time to renew and recharge, cycling in and out of work, working within our circle of control and influence, and letting go of head bangers. As Stragility leaders, we need to build our own change fitness and encourage others to do the same.

Bounce Forward from Setbacks

We talked about NASA's Death Simulations earlier in this chapter. These Death Sims also have the benefit of teaching the astronauts how to recover effectively from setbacks that may occur, and this too is important in building change fitness in our organizations.

As Jesse Thomas, CEO of Picky Bars.com and four-time Wildflower long course triathlon champion, recently shared, "When the pressure mounts and your season feels derailed, it's important to remember that you can only do what you can do. You can't control all the things that will happen or have happened. But you can determine how you react to those things and the work and preparation you put in going forward."[22] He added,

You set goals, and work hard to achieve them. Sometimes, you succeed and cel-ebrate. Other times, you fail and learn what you can from it, so you can try again. Without those failures, you don't improve, and you don't fully appreciate the successes. In the moment, it sucks, a lot. But when you persevere, and eventually achieve your goal, it makes all the sucking and suffering worth it.[23]

As change leaders, it is critical that we run water through the pipes with pilot tests and rapid prototypes so we can learn what might go wrong and what needs to be modified and thereby reduce risk when we launch. In addi-tion, by doing pre-mortems and developing contingency plans, we develop the ability to make better choices to begin with. We figure out how to pace ourselves, how to sidestep the head bangers and leverage our energy. In doing so, we develop the capability to be adaptable and bounce forward with the unexpected events that almost inevitably arise. These are essential change fitness skills that help battle change fatigue.

Learn to Learn

Peter Drucker commented, "Follow effective action with quiet reflection. From quiet reflection will come even more effective action."[24] To break the Sisyphus cycle and to achieve Stragility and change fitness, we need to get better at diagnosing and course-correcting as we go.

Dedicate Time for Learning

One thing we can do to get better at learning is after-action reviews (AARs). These learning sessions originated in the US military and are now used by com-panies like Harley-Davidson and P&G. These reviews could be organized in "I love, I wish, we should" categories or in plus/delta format, where "+" captures what was good and "delta" is what to change. Reviews might also take the form of focus groups, more open-ended input, or more detailed quantitative analyses and surveys. They might be as simple as beginning meetings with a recap of the key milestones, then doing a pulse check on progress, how people are feeling about where we are, and ideas for improvement (see Stragility Tool 5-2).

Whatever the format and process, conducting AARs creates the space to reflect, document, share, and learn and provides useful feedback for others. In addition, AARs enable us to uncover blind spots and have conversations about why we chose particular courses of action or paths, which can shed light on our underlying mindsets and how we think. These reviews also help us to understand the consequences of our decisions, figure out what we should do to realize our goals, and generate ideas for how to improve the next time around.

Introspection might include "appreciations," which companies like Whole Foods and the Container Store engage in at the start or end of meetings or projects. Appreciations are another simple but powerful tool. Each person reflects and then shares with the team something that they are grateful for in another member of the team. These types of easy-to-do introspections also foster better relationships, which fuels innovation and efficiency.

Capture and Track Stakeholder Feedback

After-action reviews help those within a project take time to reflect, but broader stakeholder pulse checks for those impacted by changes, from suppliers to customers, are also critical. Simple questions such as "What's working well and why?," "What's not and why?," and "What can be improved?" can be very powerful, as we talked about in chapter 2. Reaching out to those employees and customers who have left the organization, although sometimes painful and awkward, can also provide important insights. In addition, complementing quantitative surveys with face-to-face conversations and immersing with customers almost like an anthropologist to deeply understand their experiences offers learnings that otherwise wouldn't emerge. While massive data is beneficial, many of our clients are learning that these types of "deep dives" tend to generate more innovative improvement ideas as we've highlighted with our stories such as those of Telus, Macy's, and P&G in earlier chapters.

Connect Diverse People to Foster Reapplication

Another opportunity in many organizations stems from connecting people from different parts of the organization to share what's working that might be reapplied. Someone comes up with a fabulous idea that could be extremely beneficial in other parts of the firm but it's never shared. So another strategy for moving from change fatigue to change fitness is to connect diverse people to spark ideas and share best and next practices.

Consider the annual World Economic Forum in Davos. The World Economic Forum, which takes place every January in the snow-covered Swiss Alps, attracts 2,500 leaders in business, government, the media, and higher education. As they note, "We live in a fast-paced and interconnected world, where breakthrough technologies, demographic shifts and political transformations have far-reaching societal and economic consequences. More than ever, leaders need to share insights and innovations on how best to navigate the future. The annual meeting remains the foremost creative force for engaging the world's top leaders in collaborative activities focused on shaping the global, regional and industry agendas." By connecting diverse people globally, this forum serves to address and solve the world's greatest challenges, such as sustaining a world of nine billion, global warming, and pressing world health issues.[25]

Our organizations can also benefit from connecting diverse people. This should not be restricted to diversity of demographics: it should focus on diversity of perspective, mindset, and vantage point; across functions, levels, regions, product and service categories; and on stakeholders both inside and outside the organization. It should even encompass the so-called rebels and misfits who sometimes have the most brilliant out-of-the-box ideas.

Thus, by dedicating time to AARs, making introspection a part of every initiative and project, capturing and tracking stakeholder feedback, and connecting diverse people to foster reapplication, we continually build change capacity and capability and the change fitness needed for Stragility.

Kaiser Permanente: Building a Culture of Continuous Improvement

George Halvorson, former chairman and CEO of health giant Kaiser Permanente,[26] convincingly advocates for instilling a culture of continuous improvement. He says,

> Our culture lets our employees know that if they see a way to do something better, they should take the initiative to point it out. When a nurse in our northwest region got the idea for an automated insulin drip calculator, she spoke up – and

managed to render the old method, with its error-prone manual entries into Excel spreadsheets, obsolete. We pilot-test the most ambitious ideas at our Garfield Health Care Innovation Center, which features a simulated hospital setting as persuasive as any Hollywood set. The collective pursuit of continuous improvement is powerful not only because of the performance gains it yields, but also, I think, because it's the only cultural value that could unify an organization as large and diverse as ours. We have 180,000 staff members working on behalf of nine million members and patients. Some 57% of our employees are minorities, and only two of our eight regional presidents are white males. By emphasizing a value we share and can all act on, we create a strong sense of "us."[27]

At Kaiser Permanente, they translate ideas into action through something they call the "Innovation Consultancy." Their vision to "work with our care teams and members to bring joy and simplicity into the complex world of health" is the driver in all they do. Established over 10 years ago, the Innovation Consultancy began as an experiment to explore the "value of human centered design" in health care. At Kaiser Permanente, "this unique team brings fresh methods that liberate patients, frontline providers and managers to discover, design and implement new ways to improve the care experience of our patients and the work experience of our caregivers." Through this consultancy, they've come up with ideas such as "non-interruption sashes" so nurses administering medications aren't disrupted, mobile health vans bringing health to rural and outlying areas, and virtual physician appointments, so that people with mobility issues don't have to leave the comfort of their homes.[28]

Other companies, such as Schlumberger, a large global company that specializes in oil rigs, capture ideas and put them into action by developing mechanisms for posting and leveraging the insights. Schlumberger created something called "In Touch," their technical support service for field operators on oil rigs. In Touch is managed by dedicated experts who are available 24/7 and are tasked with keeping the information up to date and streamlined. In Touch provides solutions and advice to Schlumberger's 52,000 employees in more than 1,000 distinct locations, in over 80 countries, and in mobile service units operating 24 hours a day on drilling rigs. Schlumberger estimates that the In Touch portal has saved them over $200 million in cost savings and led to a 75 percent reduction in the time necessary to make modifications.

What does it take to cultivate a culture of continuous improvement learning? George Halvorson says,

> Three conditions must exist: People must have a rational understanding of how small improvements compound to make big differences. They must love improving – both because they are passionate about the importance of their work and because it feels so good to move to a new level of performance. And they must have enough confidence in their colleagues to believe that the organization is capable of making progress ... Every Friday afternoon for the past six years I have written a letter to all 180,000 employees celebrating a performance improvement, some great research, or a new award of that week. We celebrated when our hospitals were found to have the lowest number of pressure ulcers nationwide. (On average, 7% of hospital patients in America get them; we average below 1%. Several of our hospitals haven't seen a single pressure ulcer in more than a year.) We celebrated when the National Committee for Quality Assurance issued its latest set of quality scores, and in 29 categories Kaiser Permanente received the top score.[29]

An added bonus is that cultivating and diffusing learning through after-action reviews and stakeholder feedback also helps avoid flavor-of-the-month change initiatives, reinventing the wheel, and making the same mistakes again and again.

Recap

Organizations best able to meet the reality of constant change have a baseline of change capabilities for change fitness and work hard to maintain and sustain energy in the organization. They focus and change less to accomplish more. Recall Steve Jobs's famous focus on only four products, which still benefits Apple today. Organizations with change fitness pace and get the rhythm right like Dematic. They do pre-mortems like NASA and develop contingency plans. They energize their workforce like Google. They bounce forward from setbacks like triathlete Jesse Thomas. They cultivate learning like the military with after-action reviews. Through these methods, every change becomes a new opportunity for skill development that will strengthen Stragility and strategic fitness levels. That way they become fitter, stronger, and more resilient. They build endurance and are better able to turn potential into value-creating performance again and again, as Kaiser Permanente illustrates with its culture of continuous improvement.

STRAGILITY DIAGNOSTIC TOOL 5-1:
Creating Successful Change Again and Again:
From Change Fatigue to Change Fitness

Getting Started

Check the appropriate box:
green = good, yellow = needs work,
red = major opportunity

Green / Yellow / Red

	Green / Yellow / Red	
Do we consistently sunset projects, prioritize based on impact risk, cost, and time, and bundle our changes?	☐ ☐ ☐	**Stragility Tool 5-2 Change Fitness Processes and Practices**
Do we run water through the pipes with pilots, prototypes, pre-mortems, and contingency plans?	☐ ☐ ☐	**Stragility Tool 5-2 Change Fitness Processes and Practices**
Are we pacing work and building momentum with quick wins and milestones?	☐ ☐ ☐	**Stragility Tool 5-2 Change Fitness Processes and Practices**
Do we manage our and our organization's energy (alternating high activity with rest and recovery, building in reflection time, better eating/fitness)?	☐ ☐ ☐	**Stragility Tool 5-2 Change Fitness Processes and Practices**
Do we have ongoing feedback loops, and do we embed after-action reviews to enable us to leverage, share, and reapply our learnings from the front lines and the field to the C-suite?	☐ ☐ ☐	**Stragility Tool 5-3 After-Action Review**

STRAGILITY TOOL 5-2:
Change Fitness Processes and Practices

	What processes/ practices do we have?	What processes/practices should we have?
Change Less and Achieve More • Sunset teams, task forces, and projects • Prioritize and bundle		
Run Water through the Pipes • Set up experiments to trial, pilot, and prototype new ideas and learn • Conduct pre-mortems and contingency plans		
Pace and Get the Rhythm Right • Punctuate with quick wins and milestones • Smart timing		
Be the Change • Manage energy, not time • Remove energy drainers and avoid head bangers • Bounce forward from setbacks		
Learn to Learn • Dedicate time for introspection and after-action reviews • Connect diverse people to foster reapplication		

STRAGILITY TOOL 5-3:
After-Action Review Example

"I love ..." (what worked and why?)   "I wish ..." (challenges and why?)

"We should ..."

Key Learnings (reflections, insights, takeaways about the content of change and/or the process of change and what we'd do differently next time)

Share with whom?   How will we share?

chapter six

Putting Stragility into Action

Figure 6.1: Stragility Skills and Success Principles

Learn from the people
Plan with the people
Begin with what they have
Build on what they know
Of the best leaders
When the task is accomplished
The people all remark
We have done it ourselves.

Lao Tzu[1]

Creating Stragility requires redefining and refining strategies, building support, fostering ownership and accountability, and leading change successfully again and again. For each of these goals, we also now have concrete Stragility skills – sense and shift, embrace our inner politician, inspire and engage, and create change fitness – and their related success principles and tools that we can use to excel at strategic changes.

We've learned how companies like Macy's, Snapdeal, Starbucks, Mitsubishi, TELUS, NASA, HP, Apple, P&G, BlackRock, Alvin Ailey, Free the Children, Teranet, Kaiser Permanente, Samsø, Whole Foods, Wynn Resorts, and Dematic have excelled at strategic change transformations. And we've seen examples from manufacturing, banking, high-tech, pharmaceuticals, health, orchestras, hospitality, and the arts with headquarters in countries including the United States, Canada, France, Sweden, India, Japan, South Korea, Germany, and Australia. We've heard the wisdom of successful leaders such as George Washington and Nelson Mandela, the Dalai Lama, A.G. Lafley, Craig Kielburger, Kunal Bahl, Howard Schultz, David Novak, and so many others. We've watched how change leaders of all types have worked and reworked their approaches to create people-powered, strategic, agile organizations that have overcome huge challenges and downturns to come back strong again and again.

But what about the change challenges we are facing right now, this week, this month, this year? What if we don't have control over many of the strategic decisions in our organization or our team doesn't seem ideal. Or maybe we have insufficient resources and can't hire or fire anyone. Perhaps we're feeling overwhelmed, exhausted, scared, and demotivated. And not surprisingly, our team is feeling the same way. The only way to succeed is to tap the potential of our teams to accomplish the mission.

US Navy: Applying Stragility to *Your* Ship

That's exactly the situation Mike Abrashoff faced when he was made commander of the USS *Benfold*, a guided missile destroyer and one of the worst-performing ships in the US Navy. They were out at sea so he literally couldn't hire or fire anyone. He didn't exactly have a dream team either. They were frequently sullen and counting the days until they could get out of the Navy. So many things were out of his control. He didn't decide the missions the ship undertook. He couldn't give raises. He didn't set the budget. He was responsible for 8,600 tons of armor, four gas turbine engines, and a complex radar system. And, most importantly, he was responsible for the 310 men and women who worked on the ship.

It may sound clichéd but he discovered that change started with himself: understanding his own blind spots, how he reacted to politics and emotions, where he found inspiration, and how he energized and recharged himself. "Hard experience has taught me that real leadership is about understanding yourself first, then using that to create a superb organization. Leaders must free their subordinates to fulfill their talents to the utmost. However, most obstacles that limit people's potential are set in motion by the leader and are rooted in his or her own fears, ego needs, and unproductive habits."[2]

When he asked his team about their dreams and hopes, most didn't really have goals other than getting out of the Navy. To give people an aspirational goal, Abrashoff said they would become the "best damn ship in the Navy." This became their mantra and later what they were known as throughout the fleet. When someone visited the ship, they were greeted with, "Welcome to the best damn ship in the Navy."

The idea of achieving this goal was inspiring, but to make it happen, Abrashoff discovered he had to give up control and shift accountability to his team. As he told the crew, "It's *your* ship. You're responsible for it. Make a decision and see what happens."[3] This was hard for Abrashoff, who had to conquer his fear of shaking things up. As he said, "in business, as in the Navy, there is a general understanding that 'they' don't want rules to be questioned or challenged. For employees, the 'they' is the managers; for managers, the 'they' is the executive cadre. I worked hard at convincing my crew that I did want the rules to be questioned and challenged, and that 'they' is 'us.' One of the ways I demonstrated my commitment was to question and challenge rules to *my* bosses."[4]

He began by meeting with every single crew member and getting to know them as people – where they grew up, their favorite childhood memories, their experiences before the Navy, what they liked about their jobs, and their top gripes and their goals. Through these interviews and subsequent meetings, he came to respect the crew, see their largely untapped potential, and understand their point of view. He became their biggest cheerleader. He discovered that most people had enlisted because they needed to find a way to pay for college. Knowing this, he instituted SAT prep courses, math and English refreshers, and college courses via CD on board.

He encouraged the crew to analyze every process on the ship and ask if there was a better way to do it. Usually there was. Sure, Abrashoff had his bad days and impatient moments, but he set a goal to treat every encounter with every person on the ship as the most important thing at that moment.[5] The ability to listen, learn, inspire, respect, and see potential are Stragility skills we've seen again and again in the most effective strategic change leaders.

And he looked for early wins. For example, one of the top gripes was the quality of the food on board. Instead of Navy rations, they picked up civilian brands during port calls and sent the chefs to cooking school. The food was actually cheaper and better. They knew they had succeeded when sailors from other ships begged to come on board for lunch!

But didn't Abrashoff face the politics that are part of hierarchical organizations? Of course he did. Sometimes he had to execute orders handed down from higher-ups. Sometimes his recommendations were turned down, or worse, pocket-vetoed – there was no response at all. And quite often, he had to put up with bureaucracy beyond his control. He found his best defense against being poisoned by the politics was a strong offense. Once he realized how much he and his crew *could* influence and he started generating results, his management began to trust him. They stopped micromanaging the details and increased his and his crew's circle of control. What he discovered was that he did have the power to bring out exceptional performance in his crew. He just had to have the self-confidence to put his skills into practice.

To inspire and engage, he looked for ways to reward people and make the jobs fun. For example, when someone had a good suggestion, he'd broadcast it right away on the ship's intercom system. When he caught someone doing something good on one of his many walk-arounds, he'd hand them an award on the spot (making him far exceed his award quota according to policy!).

Once he opened up the lines of communication, the great ideas came flooding in. One resourceful sailor figured out how to convert the deck into a replica of an old drive-in movie theatre. Another noticed fuel dripping onto a very hot piece of equipment. This was extremely dangerous and could have turned into a fire that destroyed the engine room. A different crew member discovered that the vibration of the ship had caused the seals on the service heaters to crack. They wondered if other ships might be experiencing the same problem. After initial denial, it turned out the whole fleet had the same serious issue and all the ships in the fleet were serviced to fix these cracks, likely saving lives and averting major disaster.[6]

The ship's turnaround in results was both stunning and surprisingly fast. In less than two years, they excelled at every readiness indicator to become the go-to ship of the Gulf Fleet. They had the highest gunnery score in the Pacific Fleet, and they set a new record for the Navy's pre-deployment training (preparation for next assignments). And they did it all on 75 percent of their budget. It all happened because sailors were free to dream up better ways to do their jobs.

Winning with Stragility: A New, Powerful Source of Competitive Advantage

As Abrashoff's story demonstrates, winning in today's relentlessly changing business environment requires Stragility – strategic, agile, people-powered change that keeps the organization forever innovative and nimble.

Whether we're shifting strategy, embarking on a major transformation, or fine-tuning changes in the works, the ability to change successfully again and again is the ultimate core competence that will provide an enduring edge.

It all begins with you and me. To build Stragility, we must become skilled change leaders who are able to excite, enroll, and energize those around us to make change successful. As change leaders, we need to practice applying these skills. Chances are most of us are like Captain Abrashoff, initially hesitant to question previous approaches.

In this respect, change leadership is like learning to ride a bike. There's simply no substitute for just giving the approaches a try. This book is full of hands-on, practical, effective principles we can use ourselves and share across the organization. Our Stragility framework moves beyond the disparate and fragmented insights and approaches currently offered in the field to create a powerful practitioner-oriented guide and offers a full Stragility toolbox to help you get started.

Let's Get to Work

Now that we've reached the last chapter, we've got what it takes to beat the odds. With the Stragility skills, success principles, action steps, diagnostics, and tools provided, we can tap into the most powerful source of competitive advantage any organization can have – Stragility. Stragility is the ability to make this change succeed and achieve our strategy, purpose, and mission, all while building the skills and capabilities needed for the next round of changes yet to come. Stragility is the art of continuous strategic agility.

So what's the best way to get started? We suggest you go to the Stragility Diagnostic Tool 1-1 in chapter 1 to identify your key pain points, bad habits, or strategic goals that keep you up at night in current change initiatives you are engaged with or in upcoming strategic shifts you're preparing for. From there, you might then focus on the chapters related to those pain points to identify your next steps. Maybe start by working through the Stragility tools in those chapters with your team with flip charts and Post-its. A summary of all the Stragility Diagnostic Tools is provided in the appendix for your convenience. If you don't have a team, then start with chapter 3, mapping the key stakeholder groups and identifying the key influencers necessary for success that you might enroll. Then check the "At a Glance" section to remember some skills and tactics for leveraging the solutions your team generates and overcoming some of the challenges identified. Keep the process open and fluid initially to capture breakthrough ideas, and then use the Prioritization Matrices in chapter 4 to identify the highest impact, highest probability of success solutions. From there, the team may want to begin developing a mantra and stories to inspire and engage other stakeholders as the team extends its reach and incorporates broader input on what to do and the best ways to implement. All the while, you as the change leader will be building and strengthening Stragility skills, while keeping the process iterative and evolving.

Closing Thoughts

Change is hard, and achieving Stragility is always a work in progress. But it does get easier over time. Picture the tennis player Roger Federer and the scenario we talked about in the first chapter. He's just lost the first set of a major match. To get back in the game, he doesn't try to change everything at once. Instead he senses and shifts both strategy and execution to make his comeback. Sometimes he wins, sometimes he loses, but with each match he's improving his skills and applying lessons learned to win future matches.

In many ways our jobs are harder. Not only do we have to refine our strategy and execution, but we also have to navigate the politics, inspire and engage others, and make sure we as leaders and our teams have a high level of Stragility skills and change fitness to tackle the challenges we face. We have to do it again and again while juggling multiple changes simultaneously.

As Captain Abrashoff discovered, it's *our* ship and we can't and don't have to do it alone. We can start building our Stragility skills today by inviting change leaders throughout the organization to share their wisdom, creativity, innovation, and passion. We can help everyone in our organization to understand that with every change we do, we further develop this unbeatable source of competitive advantage called Stragility. So whether the seas are calm or the waves are swelling and the winds are blowing, we'll be able to unleash the power of our teams to successfully conquer even the biggest storms and simultaneously create a profound positive difference in this world.

An Invitation

Congratulations! You now have a solid understanding of Stragility and what it takes to build successful change management skills in your organization. So let's put those skills into action.

If you'd like more personalized help, we offer keynote speeches, consulting, workshops, and coaching for organizations and teams.

Visit us at www.stragilitychangemanagement.com to learn the latest on change management, download resources, hear new stories, share your own Stragility success story, or ask a question. Or contact us via email at stragility changemanagement@gmail.com.

Help us help more organizations and people like you:

- Write a review on Amazon or another online bookseller. People want to read a book that other people like.
- Tell your colleagues and friends. Post something on Facebook, LinkedIn, or Twitter.
- Apply Stragility learnings to create a change fit organization that you and others love working at.

Good luck!

Ellen Auster and Lisa Hillenbrand

Appendix:
Summary of
Stragility Diagnostic Tools

Stragility Assessment: Change Initiative _____
(insert name of your change)

STRAGILITY DIAGNOSTIC TOOL 1-1:
Pain Points, Bad Habits, Goals, and Skills

Read the whole book or look for pain points, bad habits, or strategic goals that resonate and begin there.

Pain Points	Bad Habit	Stragility Goal	Stragility Skill
Downward spirals, blindsided, strategic drift, underutilized capabilities	Lock and Load	Redefining Strategy to Win	Chapter 2: Sense and Shift
Political infighting, turf wars, resistance, apathy	Ignore the Politics	Building Support	Chapter 3: Embrace Our Inner Politician
Disengagement, blaming, inaction, resentment	Tell and Sell	Fostering Ownership and Accountability	Chapter 4: Inspire and Engage
Exhaustion, stress, burnout, wasted money, time, and resources	Change Fatigue	Creating Successful Change Again and Again	Chapter 5: Change Fitness

---

STRAGILITY DIAGNOSTIC TOOL 2-1:
Redefining Strategy to Win: From Lock and Load to Sense and Shift

Stragility Diagnostic				Getting Started

Check the appropriate box:
green = good, yellow = needs work,
red = major opportunity

Green /Yellow /Red

	Green	Yellow	Red	
Do we have a system for watching our wings for disruptive macro forces?	☐	☐	☐	**Stragility Tool 2-2 Sensing PESTE Forces**
Do we continually monitor our competitive landscape?	☐	☐	☐	**Stragility Tool 2-3 Sensing the Competitive Landscape**
Does our change strategy leverage strengths and address pain points through an understanding of root causes?	☐	☐	☐	**Stragility Tool 2-4 Internal Diagnostics and the Five Why's**
Are we clear on what winning is in our organization and what would have to be true for this change initiative to work?	☐	☐	☐	**Stragility Tool 2-5 Shifting through Backcasting**
Does everyone understand how we will measure success?	☐	☐	☐	**Stragility Tool 2-6 Measuring Success**

STRAGILITY DIAGNOSTIC TOOL 3-1:
Building Support: From Poisoned by the Politics to Embrace Our Inner Politician

Stragility Diagnostic				Getting Started
Check the appropriate box: green = good, yellow = needs work, red = major opportunity			Green /Yellow /Red	
Have we mapped the key stakeholders for this change?	☐	☐	☐	**Stragility Tool 3-2 Stakeholder Mapping**
Have we identified the key influencers and their receptivity? Do we know our sponsors, promoters, fence-sitters, and positive and negative skeptics?	☐	☐	☐	**Stragility Tool 3-3 Key Influencer Identification and Receptivity Mapping**
Are we clear on magnet factors and fear factors by stakeholder group and for our key influencers?	☐	☐	☐	**Stragility Tool 3-4 Stakeholder Engagement**
Do we have an engagement plan for engaging sponsors and promoters, fence-sitters, and positive and negative skeptics?	☐	☐	☐	**Stragility Tool 3-4 Stakeholder Engagement Also see Table 3.1 and Table 3.2**
Are we leveraging pride, developing safe language (e.g., likes and "wish for's," "yes and"), and establishing ground rules (e.g., assume positive intent, be the change) to increase likelihood that alternative points of view will be heard and new ideas incorporated?	☐	☐	☐	**Stragility Tool 3-4 Stakeholder Engagement Also see Table 3.1 and Table 3.2**
Do we have open communication channels to enable us to find common ground, gather fresh ideas, and to manage emotions explicitly?	☐	☐	☐	**Stragility Tool 3-4 Stakeholder Engagement**

STRAGILITY DIAGNOSTIC TOOL 4-1:
Fostering Ownership and Accountability: From Tell and Sell to Inspire and Engage

Stragility Diagnostic				Getting Started

Check the appropriate box: Green /Yellow /Red
green = good, yellow = needs work,
red = major opportunity

Stragility Diagnostic	Green	Yellow	Red	Getting Started
Do people understand our compelling vision, business case, and benefits of this strategic change?	☐	☐	☐	**Stragility Tool 4-2 Igniting Passion**
Are we using mantras, stories, and powerful visualizations to engage and inspire our key stakeholders in these changes?	☐	☐	☐	**Stragility Tool 4-2 Igniting Passion**
Are we building in rituals to help our people let go of the past?	☐	☐	☐	**Stragility Tool 4-3 Fostering Ownership and Accountability**
Are we facilitating our team's ability to drill down on the specifics, creating ownership, flexibility, and accountability?	☐	☐	☐	**Stragility Tool 4-3 Fostering Ownership and Accountability**
Have we brainstormed, prioritized, and filtered our ideas to come up with the best this-day-forward actions?	☐	☐	☐	**Stragility Tool 4-3 Fostering Ownership and Accountability**
Have we designed a communication strategy that is two-way, multi-channel, and engaging?	☐	☐	☐	**Stragility Tool 4-3 Fostering Ownership and Accountability**
Have we asked our stakeholders how to build the change into their work plans, measures, and incentives?	☐	☐	☐	**Stragility Tool 4-3 Fostering Ownership and Accountability**
What are we doing to provide help and hope?	☐	☐	☐	**Stragility Tool 4-3 Fostering Ownership and Accountability**

STRAGILITY DIAGNOSTIC TOOL 5-1:
Creating Successful Change Again and Again: From Change Fatigue to Change Fitness

Stragility Diagnostic				**Getting Started**

Check the appropriate box:
green = good, yellow = needs work,
red = major opportunity

Green /Yellow /Red

Do we consistently sunset projects, prioritize based on impact risk, cost, and time, and bundle our changes?	☐	☐	☐	**Stragility Tool 5-2 Change Fitness Processes and Practices**
Do we run water through the pipes with pilots, prototypes, pre-mortems, and contingency plans?	☐	☐	☐	**Stragility Tool 5-2 Change Fitness Processes and Practices**
Are we pacing work and building momentum with quick wins and milestones?	☐	☐	☐	**Stragility Tool 5-2 Change Fitness Processes and Practices**
Do we manage our and our organization's energy (alternating high activity with rest and recovery, building in reflection time, better eating/fitness)?	☐	☐	☐	**Stragility Tool 5-2 Change Fitness Processes and Practices**
Do we have ongoing feedback loops and do we embed after-action reviews to enable us to leverage, share, and reapply our learnings from the front lines and the field to the C-suite?	☐	☐	☐	**Stragility Tool 5-3 After-Action Review**

KEY FINDINGS FROM DIAGNOSTICS

Biggest Strengths (green):

Biggest Opportunities (red and yellow):

Next Steps:
(As you carve out next steps, it may be helpful to revisit the Success Principles and Action Steps found in the "At a Glance" sections at the beginning of each chapter.)

Notes

1. Stragility – Strategic, Agile, People-Powered Change

1 Peter Drucker, *Management Challenges for the 21st Century* (New York: Harper Business, 2001).

2 Chris Bradley, Angus Dawson, and Antoine Montard, "Mastering the Building Blocks of Strategy," McKinsey & Co., 1 October 2013, http://www.mckinsey .com/insights/strategy/mastering_the_building_blocks_of_strategy?p=1 (access required); "Only One-Quarter of Employers Are Sustaining Gains from Change Management Initiatives, Towers Watson Survey Finds," Towers Watson, 29 August 2013, http://www.towerswatson.com/en/Press/2013/08/Only-One -Quarter-of-Employers-Are-Sustaining-Gains-From-Change-Management; Scott Keller and Carolyn Aiken, "The Inconvenient Truth about Change Management," McKinsey & Co., 1 May 2008, http://www.mckinsey.com/app_media/reports/ financial_services/the_inconvenient_truth_about_change_management.pdf (site removed); http://www.kotterinternational.com/the-8-step-process-for -leading-change/.

3 http://fortune.com/2015/07/14/sharon-price-john-dealing-with-change/

4 A.G. Lafley, email to Lisa Hillenbrand, 1 December 2014. Used with permission.

5 Carly Fiorina, *Tough Choices: A Memoir* (New York: Penguin, 2007), 120.

2. Redefining Strategy to Win

1 Keith Hammons, "Michael Porter's Big Ideas," *Fast Company Magazine*, 1 March 2001, http://www.fastcompany.com/42485/michael-porters-big-ideas.

2 "Inspirational Quotes from Women Business Leaders," American Express OPEN Forum, 3 November 2014, http://amexopenforum.tumblr.com/ post/101679482012/inspirational-quotes-from-women-business-leaders.

3 A.G. Lafley and Roger L. Martin, *Playing to Win: How Strategy Really Works* (Boston: Harvard Business School Press, 2013).

4 "Localization with Scale: A Winning Strategy for Sustainable Profitable Growth,"
   Wilson Perumal & Company, 1 January 2011, http://www.wilsonperumal.com/
   media/publications/request_form.php?TerryLundgrenInterview, p. 6.

5 Noel Tichy, "Lafley's Legacy: From Crisis to Consumer-Driven," *Bloomberg
   Businessweek*, 10 July 2010, http://www.bloomberg.com/bw/stories/2009-06-10/
   lafleys-legacy-from-crisis-to-consumer-drivenbusinessweek-business-news-stock
   -market-and-financial-advice.

6 Barrett J. Brunsman, "Lafley: P&G to Cut About Half Its Brands," *Cincinnati
   Business Courier*, 1 August 2014.

7 Andy Atkins, "Measure for Measure: When Quantitative Meets Qualitative,"
   Rotman Management, Spring 2014: 94–6.

8 Marc deJong, Nathan Marston, and Erik Roth, "The Eight Essentials of Innovation,"
   McKinsey Quarterly, April 2015, http://www.mckinsey.com/insights/innovation/
   the_eight_essentials_of_Innovation?cid=other-eml-nsl-mip-mck-oth-1505.

9 Bill Vlasic, "Detroit's Chief Instigator," *New York Times*, B1 and B5, 24 May 2015.

10 Simon Hill, "The 11 Moments that Defined BlackBerry's Rise and Fall," 23
   September 2013, http://www.techradar.com/news/phone-and-communications/
   mobile-phones/the-10-moments-that-defined-blackberry-s-rise-and-fall-1175428.

11 Sean Silcoff, Jacquie McNish, and Steve Ladurantaye, "Inside the Fall of
   BlackBerry: How the Smartphone Inventor Failed to Adapt," *Globe and Mail*,
   27 September 2013, http://www.theglobeandmail.com/report-on-business/the
   -inside-story-of-why-blackberry-is-failing/article14563602/?page=all.

12 R. Paris, F. Lavigne, P. Wassmer, and J. Sartohadi, "Coastal Sedimentation
   Associated with the 26 December 2004 Tsunami in Lhok Nga, West Banda Aceh
   (Sumatra, Indonesia)," *Marine Geology* 238: 93–106.

13 "The Power of Knowledge: The Story of Semilieu, Indonesia," United Nations
   Office for Disaster Risk Reduction, 25 September 2007, https://www.youtube
   .com/watch?v=o175nrvTQLw.

14 Ava Seave, "Fast Followers Not First Movers Are the Real Winners," *Forbes*, 14
   October 2014, http://www.forbes.com/sites/avaseave/2014/10/14/fast
   -followers-not-first-movers-are-the-real-winners/.

15 Steve Blank, "You're Better Off Being a Fast Follower than an Originator," *Business
   Insider*, October 2010, http://www.businessinsider.com/youre-better-off-being-a
   -fast-follower-than-an-originator-2010-10#ixzz3RdmNvKMQ.

16 Jason Nazar, "The Biggest Business Blunders in History," *Business Insider*, 7
   November 2013, http://www.businessinsider.com/the-biggest-business-blunders
   -in-history-2013-11#ixzz3Ic9xck3Y.

17 http://www.cdc.gov/nchs/fastats/leading-causes-of-death.htm

18 Dan Ariely, *Predictably Irrational: The Hidden Forces that Shape Our Decisions*
   (New York: Harper Collins, 2008); Nassim Nicholas Taleb, *The Black Swan: The
   Impact of the Highly Improbable*, 2nd ed. (London: Penguin, 2010).

19 "SoftBank's Snapdeal Investment Highlights eBay's Plight in India," 29 October 2014, *Times of India*, http://info.shine.com/article/softbanks-snapdeal-investment-highlights-ebays-plight-in-india/8115.html.

20 Backcasting was first used in the environmental field. See, for example, John Holmberg and Karl-Henrik Robert, "Backcasting from Non-Overlapping Sustainability Principles – A Framework for Strategic Planning," *International Journal of Sustainable Development and World Ecology* 7 (2000): 291–308, http://www.naturalstep.org/en/backcasting.

21 Trey Popp, "The Lettuce Cure," *Pennsylvania Gazette*, May/June 2014, http://thepenngazette.com/the-lettuce-cure/.

22 Rosamund Stone Zander and Benjamin Zander, *The Art of Possibility* (Boston: Harvard Business School Press, 2000), 30.

23 Michael Robertson, "Cutting Your Losses: How to Avoid the Sunk Cost Trap," *Ivey Business Journal*, November 2009, http://iveybusinessjournal.com/publication/cutting-your-losses-how-to-avoid-the-sunk-cost-trap/.

24 Kia Kokalitcheva, "Google Says Crazy Moonshot Projects Will Ensure Its Lasting Success," *Fortune*, 3 June 2015, http://fortune.com/2015/06/03/googles-moonshots-investors/.

25 Free the Children, http://www.freethechildren.com/about-us/our-core-values/.

26 Me to We, http://www.metowe.com/about-us/our-story/.

27 Harvard professor Francis Aguilar is thought to be the creator of PEST Analysis. He included a scanning tool called ETPS in his 1967 book, *Scanning the Business Environment*. The name was later tweaked to create the current acronym (http://www.mindtools.com/pages/article/newTMC_09.htm).

3. Building Support

1 An earlier version of this chapter appeared in Ellen R. Auster and Trish Ruebottom, "Navigating the Politics and Emotions of Change," *MIT Sloan Management Review* 54, no. 4 (2013): 31–6.

2 Ravi Kant is the former Vice Chairman and Managing Director of TATA Motors India's Largest Automobile Manufacturer. Gautam Kumra, "Leading Change: An Interview with the Managing Director of Tata Motors," McKinsey & Company Insights and Publications, January 2007, http://www.mckinsey.com/insights/organization/leading_change_an_interview_with_the_managing_director_of_tata_motors.

3 Fiorina, *Tough Choices*, 200.

4 David Novak, *The Education of an Accidental CEO: Lessons Learned from the Trailer Park to the Corner Office* (New York: Three Rivers Press, 2007), 122–3.

5 Everett M. Rogers, *Diffusion of Innovations*, 3rd ed. (New York: Free Press, 1983). Rogers's diffusion curve is comprised of innovators, early adopters, the early and late majority, and laggards.

6 Malcolm Gladwell, *The Tipping Point: How Little Things Can Make a Big Difference* (Boston: Little, Brown, 2000).

7 Jeff Herbst, "President Herbst: Student Demonstration on Campus Climate," *Colgate Scene*, 7 November 2014, http://news.colgate.edu/scene/2014/11/message-from-president-herbst-2.html.

8 "What Successful Transformations Share: McKinsey Global Survey Results," McKinsey & Co., 1 January 2010, http://www.mckinsey.com/insights/organization/what_successful_transformations_share_mckinsey_global_survey_results.

9 Elsa Keslassy, "Technicolor Topper Frederic Rose Put R&D at Center of Corporate Turnaround," *Variety*, 4 November 2014, http://variety.com/2014/film/news/technicolor-topper-frederic-rose-put-rd-at-center-of-corporate-turnaround-1201346544/.

10 Douglas A. Ready, Linda A. Hill, and Robert J. Thomas, "Building a Game-Changing Talent Strategy," *Harvard Business Review* 92, nos. 1–2 (January–February 2014): 62–8.

11 Aaron De Smet, Johanne Lavoie, and Elizabeth Schwartz Hjoe, "Developing Better Change Leaders," McKinsey & Co., April 2012, http://www.mckinsey.com/insights/organization/developing_better_change_leaders.

12 "Nelson Mandela Online," *Quotes, Biography, Autobiography, Movies and Pictures of Nelson Mandela*, http://www.nelsonmandelaonline.net/#sthash.7xmVTR0E.dpuf.

13 Michael M. Kaiser, *The Art of the Turnaround: Creating and Maintaining Healthy Arts Organizations* (Hanover, NH: University Press of New England, 2008), xii.

14 Ibid., 59.

15 Ibid., 50.

16 Ibid., xiii.

17 D. Michael Abrashoff, *It's Your Ship: Management Techniques from the Best Damn Ship in the Navy* (New York: Warner Books, 2002), 47.

18 Søren Hermansen, "Renewable Island Director: We Need the Opposite of Energy Union," EurActiv, 16 March 2015, http://www.euractiv.com/sections/energy/renewable-island-director-we-need-opposite-energy-union-312903.

19 Søren Hermansen, "Commonity = common + community," TEDx Copenhagen Salon, December 2013, https://www.youtube.com/watch?v=G-xFXOJNxAQ.

20 Diane Cardwell, "Green-Energy Inspiration Off the Coast of Denmark," *New York Times*, 17 January 2015, http://www.nytimes.com/2015/01/18/business/energy-environment/green-energy-inspiration-from-samso-denmark.html?_r=1; Diane Cardwell, "Fueled by Danish Ingenuity," *PowerSource: Energy News, In Context*, 17 January 2015, http://powersource.post-gazette.com/powersource/latest-alternative-energy/2015/01/17/Fueled-by-Danish-Ingenuity/stories/201501170134.

21 Hermansen, "Commonity = common + community."

4. Fostering Ownership and Accountability

1   Elizabeth Lesser, *Broken Open: How Difficult Times Can Help Us Grow* (New York: Villard, 2005), xviii.
2   Rosabeth Moss Kanter, *The Change Masters* (New York: Simon and Schuster, 1984), 64.
3   "2012 Global Workforce Study Engagement at Risk: Driving Strong Performance in a Volatile Global Environment," Towers Watson, 1 July 2012, http://www .towerswatson.com/Insights/IC-Types/Survey-Research-Results/2012/07/2012 -Towers-Watson-Global-Workforce-Study.
4   John E. Pepper, email to Lisa Hillenbrand, 29 July 2014; permission for use granted.
5   Takeo Yamaguchi, "Voices from the Front Lines," *Harvard Business Review*, September 2014, https://hbr.org/2014/09/voices-from-the-front-lines.
6   The story "Smooth Sailing" was developed after a series of interviews with the person who led this project and a review of his internal documents and launch materials. The company has asked to remain anonymous.
7   Fiorina, *Tough Choices*, 115.
8   Ibid., 123–4.
9   "Our Values and Mission," Whole Foods Market, http://www.wholefoodsmarket .com/careers/our-values-and-mission.
10 John P. Kotter and Dan S. Cohen, *The Heart of Change: Real-Life Stories of How People Change Their Organizations* (Boston: Harvard Business School Press, 2002).
11 Peter Fuda and Richard Badham, "Fire, Snowball, Mask, Movie: How Leaders Spark and Sustain Change," *Harvard Business Review* 89, no. 11 (2011): 145–8; Peter Guber, *Tell to Win: Connect, Persuade, and Triumph with the Hidden Power of Story* (New York: Crown Business, 2011).
12 "2012 Global Workforce Study Engagement at Risk: Driving Strong Performance in a Volatile Global Environment," Towers Watson, 1 July 2012, http://www .towerswatson.com/Insights/IC-Types/Survey-Research-Results/2012/07/2012 -Towers-Watson-Global-Workforce-Study; R. Edward Freeman, "Business Is about Purpose: R. Edward Freeman at TEDxCharlottesville 2013," YouTube, 1 January 2013, https://www.youtube.com/watch?v=7dugfwJthBY; Rajendra S. Sisodia, Jagdish N. Sheth, and David B. Wolfe, *Firms of Endearment: How World-Class Companies Profit from Passion and Purpose*, 2nd ed. (Upper Saddle River, NJ: Pearson FT Press, 2014); Robert Musselwhite, "How Companies Can Profit From Doing Good," *Fast Company*, June 20, 2014, http://www.fastcompany .com/3032059/bottom-line/how-companies-can-profit-from-doing-good.
13 Fuda and Badham, "Fire, Snowball, Mask, Movie," 145–8; and Guber, *Tell to Win*.
14 "Wynn Resorts: The King of Vegas," *60 Minutes*, 12 April 2009.

15 Leslie Fieger, "Attitude Is Everything?" http://www.lesliefieger.com/articles/attitude_is_everything.htm.
16 "What Successful Transformations Share: McKinsey Global Survey Results."
17 Brenda Zimmerman, "Thrive! Engaging with Complexity," Keynote Summit: Thrive, Nova Scotia, 23 October 2014, https://www.youtube.com/watch?v=hUWiFoazeX0.
18 Jean-Jacques Brousson, *Anatole France en pantoufles* (Paris: Les Editions G. Grès, 1924).
19 Fiorina, *Tough Choices*, 121.
20 http://www.diversityinc.com/novartis-pharmaceuticals-corporation/
21 "CCTS Report Reaffirms TELUS' Position as Telecom Industry's Customer Service Leader," TELUS, 4 November 2014, http://about.telus.com/community/english/news_centre/news_releases/blog/2014/11/04/ccts-report-reaffirms-telus-position-as-telecom-industry-s-customer-service-leader.
22 Ibid.; http://sustainability.telus.com/en/customers_first/customers_first.
23 "CCTS Report Reaffirms TELUS' Position as Telecom Industry's Customer Service Leader."
24 Howard Schultz and Dori Jones Yang, *Pour Your Heart into It: How Starbucks Built a Company One Cup at a Time* (New York: Hyperion, 1997), xx.
25 http://www.unileverusa.com/aboutus/ourvision/
26 Novak, *The Education of an Accidental CEO*, xx.
27 Stevie Smith, *Collected Poems* (New York: New Directions Publishing, 1983), 393–6.
28 Brenda Zimmerman, "Preventing Snapback: The Challenge of Resilient Systems," Collective Impact Summit, Toronto, 6–10 October 2014, https://www.youtube.com/watch?v=cnXRX0Y9io8.
29 Our deepest thanks to Marc Sykes, Strategy and Operations leader at Teranet, for sharing this story.
30 "The Soldiers and the Trench Story," Businessballs, http://www.businessballs.com/stories.htm.
31 Howard Schultz and Joanne Gordon, *Onward: How Starbucks Fought for Its Life without Losing Its Soul* (New York: Rodale, 2011), 153.
32 Adrian Lee, "A Growing Culture War," *Maclean's*, 21 July 2014, pp. 38–9; Aaron Pressman, "Coffee Wars IV – Schultz Rallies Starbucks' Baristas," *Bloomberg Businessweek*, 22 February 2007, http://www.bloomberg.com/bw/stories/2007-02-22/coffee-wars-iv-schultz-rallies-starbucks-baristas.
33 Schultz and Gordon, *Onward*, 193.
34 Ibid., 195, 75.
35 Ibid., 241.
36 Ibid., 75.
37 Ibid., 258.

38 Ibid., 98.
39 Howard Schultz, "Howard Schultz Transformation Agenda Communication #1," Starbucks Newsroom, https://news.starbucks.com/news/howard-schultz -transformation-agenda-communication-1.

5. Creating Successful Change

1 Susan Scott, *Fierce Conversations*: *Achieving Success at Work and in Life One Conversation at a Time* (New York: Berkley Publishing Group, 2002), 125.
2 A.A. Milne, *The World of Pooh* (New York: E.P. Dutton, 1957), 7.
3 Shandra Martinez, "Dematic Isn't Your Dad's Rapistan: Why That Is Good for Grand Rapids," Mlive.com, 20 February 2014, http://www.mlive.com/business/ west-michigan/index.ssf/2014/02/dematic_isnt_your_dads_rapista.html.
4 Samantha Grossman, "This Video Is Proof that Southwest Flight Attendants Are the Sassiest People of All Time," *Time*, 20 June 2014, http://time.com/2905696/ heres-proof-that-southwest-flight-attendants-are-the-sassiest-people-of-all -time/.
5 Joan Lewis, email to Lisa Hillenbrand, 7 February 2015.
6 Walter Isaacson, *Steve Jobs* (New York: Simon & Schuster, 2011), 337–9.
7 "Q&A with Costco's CEO, W. Craig Jelinek: You Asked Costco's Chief: Why No Express Lanes?," *Consumer Reports*, December 2014, 10.
8 http://blog.us.playstation.com/2013/10/30/ps4-the-ultimate-faq-north-america/ comment-page-31/
9 G. Klein, "Performing a Project Pre-mortem," *Harvard Business Review* 85, no. 9 (2007): 18–19.
10 Chris Hadfield, *An Astronaut's Guide to Life on Earth* (New York: Random House, 2013).
11 Fiorina, *Tough Choices*, 271.
12 Nelson Mandela, *Long Walk to Freedom: The Autobiography Nelson Mandela* (Boston: Little Brown, 1995), 751.
13 "Louis Carter – Best Practice Institute," Louis Carter, http://louiscarter.com/.
14 Tony Schwartz, "Relax! You'll Be More Productive," *New York Times*, 9 February 2013, http://www.nytimes.com/2013/02/10/opinion/sunday/relax-youll-be -more-productive.html?pagewanted=all&_r=1.
15 Marcia Conner, "Advice for Executives: Get Some Sleep!," Fast Company, http:// www.fastcompany.com/919187/advice-executives-get-some-sleep.
16 Schwartz, "Relax! You'll Be More Productive."
17 "What Successful Transformations Share: McKinsey Global Survey Results."
18 "Stanford Study Finds Walking Improves Creativity," Stanford University, 1 April 2014, http://news.stanford.edu/news/2014/april/walking-vs-sitting-042414.
19 Doreen Carvajal, "Writing Retreat by Rail," *New York Times*, 26 October 2014.

20 Shareen Pathak, "Droga5 Is No. 4 on Ad Age's 2014 Agency A-List," Advertising Age Special Report Agency, 3 February 2014, http://adage.com/article/special -report-agency-alist-2014/droga5-4-ad-age-s-2014-agency-a-list/291300/.
21 Sidney Piburn, *The Dalai Lama: A Policy of Kindness* (Delhi: Motilal Banarsidass, 2002), 40.
22 Jesse Thomas, "Triathlife with Jesse Thomas: The Not So Perfect Season," *Triathlete*, 1 November 2014.
23 Jesse Thomas, "2012 70.3 World Champs Race Report," Leap Day Sports, September 2012, http://leapdaysports.com/2012/09/12/2012-70-3-world -champs-race-report/.
24 http://www.druckerinstitute.com/2011/02/high-time-for-think-time/
25 "WEF Institutional Brochure 2014," World Economic Forum, 2014, http://www3 .weforum.org/docs/WEF_InstitutionalBrochure_2014.pdf.
26 George C. Halvorson, "The Culture to Cultivate," *Harvard Business Review* 91, nos. 7–8 (July–August 2013): 34; and Jayne O'Donnell, "The Kaiser Way: Lesson for U.S. Health Care?" *USA Today*, 7 August 2014, http://www.usatoday.com/story/ news/nation/2014/08/06/kaiser-permanente-obamacare-accountable-care -organizations-hospitals/12763591/.
27 Halvorson, "The Culture to Cultivate."
28 "Design for Joy," Kaiser Permanente Innovation Consultancy: Projects, https:// xnet.kp.org/innovationconsultancy/aboutus.html; https://www.advisory.com/ daily-briefing/2011/08/29/do-not-disturb-nurses; http://share.kaiserpermanente .org/article/kaiser-permanente-unveils-the-nations-most-wired-mobile-health -vehicle/; http://www.californiahealthline.org/picture-of-health/2014/how -many-virtual-doctor-visits-were-conducted-at-kaiser-permanente-northern -california.
29 Halvorson, "The Culture to Cultivate," 34.

6. Putting Stragility into Action

1 Lao Tzu, quoted in Richard Pascale, Jerry Sternin, and Monique Sternin, *The Power of Positive Deviance: How Unlikely Innovators Solve the World's Toughest Problems* (Cambridge, MA: Harvard Business School Press, 2010), 193.
2 Abrashoff, *It's Your Ship*, 4.
3 Ibid., 6.
4 Ibid., 7.
5 Ibid., 44.
6 Ibid., 70.

Index